Max Planck   Moritz Schlick

Positivism and the Real External World

Positivism and Realism

With an Introduction by Michael J. Shaffer

Planck's paper is translated by
Fritz Lewertoff and André Michaud
Schlick's paper is translated by Peter Heath

MINKOWSKI
Institute Press

Max Karl Ernst Ludwig Planck
23 April 1858 – 4 October 1947

Friedrich Albert Moritz Schlick
14 April 1882 – 22 June 1936

ISBN: 978-1-927763-84-1 (softcover)
ISBN: 978-1-927763-85-8 (ebook)

Minkowski Institute Press
Montreal, Quebec, Canada
http://minkowskiinstitute.org/mip/

For information on all Minkowski Institute Press publications
visit our website at http://minkowskiinstitute.org/mip/books/

PUBLISHER'S PREFACE

This volume includes the first English translation of Max Planck's 1930 lecture "Positivism and the Real External World"[1] (translated by Fritz Lewertoff and André Michaud) and a new publication of Moritz Schlick's response "Positivism and Realism" (1932).[2]

Planck's and Schlick's papers were typeset in LaTeX and noticed typos in the texts were corrected.

18 July 2020   Minkowski Institute Press

---

[1]M. Planck, *Positivismus und reale Aussenwelt*. (Akademische Verlagsgesellschaft, Leipzig 1931).

[2]M. Schlick, "Positivismus und Realismus," *Erkenntnis*, Volume 3 (1932), pp. 1-31. Translated into English by Peter Heath and published in Moritz Schlick, *Philosophical Papers*, Volume II (1925-1936, edited by Henk L. Mulder Mulder and Barbara F.B. van de Velde-Schlick (D. Reidel Publishing Company, Dordrecht 1979), pp. 259-284.

ii

INTRODUCTION

Michael J. Shaffer

1. Introduction

This book contains an original translation of Max Planck's 1931 *Positivismus und reale Aussenwelt* and Moritz Schlick's 1932 response, first published in the journal *Erkenntnis*. While the latter work has been widely read — due largely to its inclusion in Ayer's well known 1959 edited collection *Logical Positivism* — the former work has not been widely read. Planck's book is a tidied-up version of a lecture delivered on November 12, 1930 and it was published as a pamphlet by Akademische Verlagsgesellschaft in 1931. But, this critical plank in Planck's defense of realism was not itself widely accessible until now. This all makes for a rather one-sided understanding of Planck's and Schlick's debate about realism and positivism where Planck is supposed to have misunderstood Schlick's views.[1] So, this volume is intended to make both sides of the debate accessible in one place. It is an important chapter in the long-running debate about the possibility of knowledge of the external world and it is an important precursor both to the protocol sentence debate and to the contemporary debate about scientific realism.[2]

To properly understand this important episode in the philosophy of science and epistemology it is important to set

---

[1]See, for example, Friedman 1997 and Oberdan 2009 and 2015.

[2]See Carnap 1932, Schlick 1934, Neurath 1932/1933 and Leplin 1984.

iii

the context of the debate. Max Planck received the Nobel Prize in physics for his role in the development of quantum mechanics in 1918, but it is entirely anachronistic to suppose that Planck's interests only involved work in pure physics. The tendency to impose more recent and distinctly more rigid disciplinary divisions on the history of science and philosophy obscures the fact that many thinkers that were deeply involved in the development of modern physics were also deeply involved in debates about the methodology of the sciences and epistemology. All one needs to do is look at the wide-scoped works of Planck's contemporaries to see that this is true. Planck himself is no exception to this point and he wrote extensively on the philosophy of science, especially in his later years. Importantly, his philosophical work was deeply influenced by his teacher Hermann von Helmholtz and this is germane to the Planck/Schlick exchange. What is crucial to understand first about this exchange is that Planck and Schlick had very similar views in many respects that were derived from the Kantian tradition that was prominent in German philosophy prior to the 1930's.[3] They were both empiricists whose work addressed the crucial difference between knowledge and acquaintance that had been a central theme in Russell's positivism in the first two decades of the twentieth century and they were both acutely aware of the role of conventions in systems of knowledge that had become a matter of great importance given the work of Einstein and Poincaré.[4] But, the central dispute that arose between them in the two works presented here had to do with their differing understandings of the nature of perception and the possibility of empirical knowledge of reality as it is in itself.

---

[3]See Coffa 1991, Friedman 1992, Friedman 1999 and Friedman 2001 on this point.

[4]See Schlick 1915, Einstein 1916, Russell 1912, Russell 1914, Russell 1918 and Russell 1922, and Poincaré 1905.

2. The Rise of Positivism in Germany and the Planck/Schlick Debate

Planck's philosophical views influenced many thinkers associated with the Berlin Circle (headed by Hans Reichenbach) and the Vienna circle (headed by Moritz Schlick). In turn, however, his own views were influenced by the work of the members of both groups. Generally, Planck's views reflect the move away from the prevailing Kantianism that antedated the rise of positivism in the early 20th century in Europe, though his views reflect a serious engagement with Kantian philosophy, and the influence of Helmholtz's naturalism and realism. His approach to philosophy and science and its similarities to the thinking of Reichanbach and Schlick is not a surprising one given that Planck directed Schlick's doctorate in Berlin and given that Planck, along with Einstein, also helped to secure a position for Reichenbach at the University of Berlin. Of course, Schlick ultimately helped to develop the logical positivism that influenced Reichenbach's views, but they could not avoid being influenced by Planck's own thinking given Planck's role in their academic lives. So, Planck was directly familiar with the work of the members of the Berlin and Vienna Circles, particularly Reichenbach's and Schlick's views, and he shared the same Kantian background with them. First, it is of special importance here to recognize that all three of these thinkers were acutely aware of the crucial difference that Kant had made between the possibilities of knowledge of phenomena and of knowledge of noumena. Second, they were keenly aware of Kant's view, spelled out in detail in the *Prolegomena to any Future Metaphysics* (1783) and earlier in *The Critique of Pure Reason* (1781), that scientific metaphysics cannot be anything more than the study of the necessary categorical structure of thought and the forms of intuition.

In any case, against this background, it is crucial to note that the Berlin Circle was greatly influential in the intellectual scene in Berlin at the time when Planck wrote his core works on philosophy. The view of science and philosophy that he ultimately espouses is very similar in some important respects to Reichenbach's Kantian-inspired views presented in his *The Theory of Relativity and A Priori Knowledge*, originally published in 1920 and Reichenbach's later 1938 book *Experience and Prediction*, which reflects Reichenbach's own mature realism. Planck, like Reichanbach, was a scientific realist and he opposed the anti-metaphysical logical positivism endorsed by Schlick and the sort of pure empiricism endorsed by Mach.[5] So, while the philosophical atmosphere in Berlin in the 1930s was steeped in the rise of empiricistic positivism, Planck objected to what he took to be one of the foundations of positivism, i.e. its alleged adoption of a form of phenomenalistic anti-realism. This was such a bone of contention that Planck thought it necessary to criticize Machian positivism in the celebrated section 4 of his 1925 *A Survey of Physical Theory* titled "The Unity of the Physical Universe." Later, Planck explicitly addressed at length Schlick's own positivism in *Positivismus und reale Aussenwelt* and in chapter 2 of his 1932 book *Where is Science Going?* It is then perfectly clear that Planck took this methodological issue to be one that was deeply important, despite his sharing with Schlick a commitment to empiricism and a commitment to the Kantian idea that knowledge requires conceptualization. In order, however, to see what Planck found specifically objectionable about Schlick's positivism, we need to get a rather more detialed perspective on both Planck's and Schlick's views of science and epistemology. Let us then begin then with Planck's views.

3. Planck's Realism

In his 1936 book *Philosophy of Physics* Planck defends

---

[5]See Oberdan 2015, Oberdan 2017 and Friedman 1999.

the view that science and philosophy cannot be neatly disentangled. Given Planck's Kantian leanings, this is principally because philosophy concerns itself with the possibility of all knowledge and so must encompass knowledge of physics and the rest of the sciences. But, he also held that any reasonable philosophical system must not conflict with what we have learned about nature via science, for otherwise it would go against our best knowledge of the nature of reality. So, these two epistemic domains are inter-dependent as Planck sees it. Moreover, on this basis we must be careful not to hold philosophical principles to be a priori dictates that would shackle science and we must be careful to understand that science requires a philosophical underpinning. Put simply, Planck saw that physics and the other sciences cannot be practiced in isolation from general philosophy. *All* physical theories presuppose some philosophical framework or principles of classification, but, *pace* Kant, there is no single a priori true framework or principle of classification that must be assumed as a matter of necessity. Such principles stand above the scientific theory and shape how we see and investigate the world, but, given Einstein's and Poincaré's revolutionary introduction of relativity, there are many such frameworks that could be adopted. Planck then held that the adoption of any philosophical framework requires making a value judgment concerning the appropriateness of that framework for the guidance of scientific research and as a set of presuppositions about both methodology and reality. This includes adopting familiar methodological values like respect for truth and commitments to principles like that of causality and the basic concept of a physical object. It is in virtue of this fact that Planck sees that every physical theory presupposes some philosophical system of concepts and he held that one of the core presuppositions of empirical science is the commitment to realism. This latter commitment is crucial, as the failure to appreciate this would turn science into a purely subjective endeavour.

Given this understanding of science, Planck asserted that many bitter scientific controversies are really just disputes about the selection of principles of classification or frameworks, rather than disputes about purely empirical matters. This is especially important because, given the influence of Einstein, Planck believed that judgments concerning which philosophical framework to adopt are matters of conventions guided by purely pragmatic implications. Different scientists or scientific communities can, at least in principle, approach empirical inquiry differently in terms of different assumed frameworks grounded in different value judgments even if they are not aware of this. So, it is of the utmost importance *both* that scientists concern themselves with the search for truth and that scientists concern themselves with the search for correct values. There simply is no science practiced independently of philosophy, and specifically independently of both conventional principles of classification and values. In other words, scientists should not pretend that empirical science is free of presuppositions and scientists should not pretend that science does not require philosophical support. But, he is also clear that if these varied ways of understanding the empirical world are to be scientific, then they must assume realism.

Planck's way of looking at science and its philosophical presuppositions then suggests that there can be importantly different kinds of conflicts between belief systems involving empirical theories. There can be disputes about the non-empirical philosophical frameworks associated with empirical theories and there can be disputes about empirical theories framed in terms of the same non-empirical philosophical framework. Importantly, as Planck sees it, the first kind of dispute can be resolved only by appeal to the pragmatic implications associated with the conflicting frameworks, whereas conflicts of the second sort can be resolved by appeal to the empirical basis of science (i.e. measurements). Where we have conflicts of the first sort we can then only look at the conventional frameworks adopted and then consider the consequences they entail and how we pragmatically value them. So, as we have already noted, this view involves the rejection of Kant's idea of the fixed and a priori warranted categories of though and the forms of sense and replaces it with the idea that all science is conducted in terms of some contingently adopted philosophical framework or other. But, the selection of any such framework is a non-empirical matter (i.e. a convention). So, Planck's view is very nearly identical to Reichenbach's adoption of what has come to be called the relativized a priori and its supposed role in the conduct of science.[6]

Reichenbach too held that all scientific theories are presented in conjunction with a philosophical framework that makes the empirical application of that theory possible and that such philosophical frameworks are not selected on the basis of empirical considerations.[7] However, Planck coupled this sort of view with a thorough-going empiricism based on Helmholz's causal theory of perception and this yielded a theory of science that stressed both the limits of empiricism and the role of philosophical presuppositions in scientific frameworks. It is on this basis that Planck saw that one could potentially synthesize Kantian and realist themes. Observations yield up understanding of systematic structural relations caused by objects conceived in terms of a conventionally adopted framework and it in this manner that we can transcend the unified structure of appearances.[8] While the nature of our percepts is not knowable objectively and things in themselves might not resemble those percepts, the relations among them are objectively discernable by careful empirical enquiry.

---

[6]See Friedman 2001.
[7]See Shaffer 2011 for critical discussion of this view.
[8]Oberdan 2015.

x

4. Schlick's Positivism

Moritz Schlick began his work in physics, though he ultimately assumed the Chair of *Naturalphilosophie* in Vienna in
1922. As noted earlier, Schlick's 1904 doctorate in physics was
directed by Planck in Berlin and Schlick was thus introduced
to a philosophically rich approach to physics. His first book,
Space and Time in Contemporary Physics, was published in
1917. It laid out an interpretation of Einstein's general theory of relativity that was warmly welcomed by Einstein himself. But, the deep philosophical problems associated with
the new physics led Schlick to switch his focus from physics
to more pure and traditional philosophical problems. To this
end, he published his *General Theory of Knowledge* in 1918
and this shift in focus was consciously made under the aegis
of the recognition that Einstein's theories had deeply serious
implications for the Kantian framework that took Newtonian
mechanics to be a priori true of space and time. Schlick's early
work in epistemology then was concerned with the Kantian
problem of the relationship between perception and conceptual knowledge and with the conventional nature of concepts
that followed from relativity theory. In this stage of his work,
Schlick defended the position that knowledge cannot be had
by acquaintance and that all knowledge involved subsuming
perceptual contents under some system of concepts. But,
when this problem in contextualized in terms of the conventional nature of concepts that follows from relativity, we are
left with the problem that no single system of concepts can
be said to be a priori true.

So, Schlick adopted the position that systems of concepts
were adopted as mere conventions. Via Einstein's influence,
this led to Schlick's correspondence with Reichenbach concerning the relativized a priori and its role in physical theory.[9] Schlick adamantly denied that there were any a priori

---

[9]See Oberdan 2009.

truths and so appeared to be at odds with Reichanbach. However, following their correspondence, ultimately Schlick came to the recognition that his differences with Reichenbach were largely terminological. In other words, Reichenbach's relativized a priori claims are just Schlick's philosophical conventions.[10] Notice too that this position is essentially the same position defended by Planck about the role of concepts in scientific theories.[11] So, on this matter Planck, Schlick and Reichenbach were really in agreement.

It is clear then that the dispute between Planck and Schlick has more to do with the nature of perception and the matter of realism, but, as we shall see, the matter is complex. Moreover, this matter is made more complicated by the fact that Schlick's thinking had taken a fairly dramatic turn away from his early more Kantian views by the 1930s, largely due to the influence of Wittegenstein's and Carnap's works.[12] By 1932, when Schlick's response to Planck was published, Schlick had developed much of the sort of logical positivism that is characteristic of the Vienna Circle and, on the basis of the verification principle, it had at its core the rejection of metaphysics as meaningless. The verification principle simply said that the meaning of an expression is its (possible) method of verification by observation statements and so claims that were in principle unverifiable by appeal to observation sentences were deemed to be meaningless. This ultimately caused serious problems for Schlick's empiricist views on the perceptual basis of science and his early view that there can be no knowledge by acquaintance. Given the anti-metaphysical stance of his later positivism, it was not just that there can be no knowledge by perceptual acquaintance, but rather that the whole of Helmholtz's causal theory of perception (and

---

[10]See Schlick 1920a, 1920b and 1920c, Reichenbach 1920, Einstein 1915, Einstein 1916, Einstein 1920, Oberdan 2017 and Shaffer 2011.

[11]Shaffer 2011.

[12]See Wittgenstein 1922 and Carnap 1928.

any other similar view) was meaningless in terms of the verification principle. We simply cannot know from where and how observation sentences come about. In point of fact, the very question of realism vs. anti-realism was, as the mature Schlick saw it, meaningless. So, we cannot ever know that the content of our observations sentences and their relations do/do not resemble things in themselves and their relations. As such, there can be no knowledge of reality in itself of any sort for Schlick. In good Carnapian fashion, Schlick adopted the view that various empirically equivalent systems of empirical knowledge are simply reductions of theoretical claims to basic statements that we call observation statements in virtue of their particular syntactic features. So, the exchange between Planck and Schlick reproduced here then anticipates the infamous protocol sentences controversy that soon followed between Schlick and Neurath.[13] It is then also here that we can begin to see where Planck objects to Schlick's views and why Schlick takes Planck to have misunderstood him. Specifically, as the two essay reproduced here demonstrate, it originates with a deep difference in their perspectives on theoretical knowledge and how it relates to perception.

References

Carnap, R. (1928). *The Logical Structure of the World*. Berkeley: The University of California Press.

Carnap. R. (1932). "Über Protocolsätze," *Erkenntnis* 3: 215-228.

Coffa, A. (1991). *The Semantic Tradition from Kant to Carnap*. Cambridge: Cambridge University Press.

---

[13] See Carnap 1932, Schlick 1934 and Neurath 1932/1933.

Einstein, A. (1915). Letter to Moritz Schlick, December 14, 1915, Einstein Collection, Hebrew University, EC 21620.

Einstein, A. (1916). "Die Grundlage der allgemeinen Relativitätstheorie," *Annalen der Physik*, 49: 769-822.

Einstein, A. (1920). Letter to Moritz Schlick, April 19, 1920, Einstein Collection, Hebrew University, EC 21633.

Friedman, M. (1992). *Kant and the Exact Sciences*. Cambridge: Harvard University Press.

Friedman, M. (1997). "Helmholtz' *Zeichentheorie* and Schlick's *Allgemeine Erkenntnislehre*: Early Logical Empiricism and its Nineteenth-Century Background," Philosophical Topics 25: 19–50.

Friedman, M. (1999). *Reconsidering Logical Positivism*. Cambridge: Cambridge University Press.

Friedman, M. (2001). *The Dynamics of Reason*. Stanford: CSLI.

Helmholtz, H. (1924-5). *Treatise on Physiological Optics*. Milwaukee: Optical Society of America.

Helmholtz. H. (1977). *Epistemological Writings*. Dordrecht: D. Reidel.

Leplin, J. (1984). *Scientific Realism*. Berkeley: University of California Press.

Neurath, O. (1932/1933). "Protocolsätze," *Erkenntnis* 3: 204-214.

Oberdan, T. (2009). "Geometry, Convention, and the Relativized *A priori*: The Schlick-Reichenbach Correspondence," in Stadler, et al. *Stationen, Dem Philosophern und Physiker Moritz Schlick*. Vienna: Springer, 186–211.

Oberdan, T. (2015). "From Helmholz to Schlick: The Evolution of the Sign-theory of Perception," *Studies in the History and Philosophy of Science* 52: 35-43.

Oberdan, T. (2017). "Moritz Schlick," *The Stanford Encyclopedia of Philosophy* (Winter 2017 Edition), Edward N. Zalta (ed.), `https://plato.stanford.edu/archives/win2017/entries/schlick/`.

Planck, M. (1931). *Positivismus und reale Aussenwelt.* Leipzig: Akademische Verlagsgesellschaft.

Planck, M. (1933). *Where is Science Going?* London: George Allen and Unwin.

Poincare, H. (1905). *Science and Hypothesis.* London: Scott.

Reichenbach, H. (1920). *The Theory of Relativity and A Priori Knowledge.* Los Angeles: University of California Press.

Russell, B. (1912). *The Problems of Philosophy.* London: Oxford University Press.

Russell, B. (1914). "On the Nature of Acquaintance," *The Monist* 24: 1-16.

Russell, B. (1918). *The Philosophy of Logical Atomism.* Chicago: Open Court.

Russell, B. (1922). *Our Knowledge of the External World.* London: Allen and Unwin.

Schlick, M. (1920a). *Space and Time in Contemporary Physics.* Oxford: Clarendon Press.

Schlick, M. (1920b). Letter to Hans Reichenbach, September 25, 1920, *Archives for Scientific Philosophy*, No. 015–63–23.

Schlick, M. (1920c). Letter to Hans Reichenbach, November

26, 1920, *Archives for Scientific Philosophy*, No. 015-63-22.

Schlick, M. (1925). *General Theory of Knowledge*. New York: Springer Verlag.

Schlick, M. (1932). "Positivismus und Realismus," *Erkenntnis* 3: 1–31.

Schlick, M. (1934). "Über das Fundament der Erkenntnis," *Erkenntnis* 4: 79–99.

Shaffer, M. (2011). "The Constitutive A Priori and Epistemic Justification," in *What Place for the A Priori?* M. Veber and M. J. Shaffer (eds.). Chicago: Open Court, 193-210

Wittgenstein, L. (1922). *Tractatus Logico-Philosophicus*. New York: Humanities Press.

xvi

CONTENTS

1 POSITIVISM AND THE REAL EXTERNAL WORLD

by Max Planck

A talk given by Max Planck on November 12, 1930, published in Max Planck, *Positivismus und reale Aussenwelt* (Akademische Verlagsgesellschaft, Leipzig 1931)

Translated by Fritz Lewertoff and André Michaud

Ladies and Gentlemen,

We live in a strange world. Looking around, with regard to the mental and material culture in all areas, we are living in a time of extreme crises which affects our entire private and public lives with numerous signs of unrest and uncertainty. Some people want to see in this the beginning of a great upward trend whereas others interpret these signs as the harbinger of an inevitable decline. As in religion and art for a long time, there is now also in science hardly a principle that is not doubted by someone, hardly some nonsense that is not believed by someone, and this raises the question whether there is at all still one truth left which in general is valid and irrefutable and offers firm support against the all embracing waves of skepticism. Logic alone, as we accept it in its purest form, is unable to help us because if logic as such is to be looked at as unarguably certain, even then, it

1

2

cannot do more than knotting things together. For logic to become substantially meaningful it nevertheless needs a fixed starting point because even the strongest chain will not provide reliable support unless it is attached to a fixed and safe location.

Where can we find a secure location to use as a starting point to conceive nature and our world? This question may well draw our attention to the most exact of the natural sciences, namely, physics. Yet, physics too could not escape from the all-pervasive crisis. Even in the field of physics some uncertainty arose, partial opinions about theoretical questions of knowledge diverge now considerably. The already well established principles in physics, even causality as such, are randomly thrown overboard. Yes, that something like this can happen, especially with regard to physics, some may think this to be a symptom of the unreliability of human knowledge. As a physicist, and from the standpoint arrived at through my science, allow me to make some comments regarding the present state of physics with respect to the already raised questions. From this, perhaps some conclusions will come to light which are also relevant to other fields of human mind activity.

I

The source of all knowledge, and hence the origin of every science as well, lies in personal experiments. Everyone assimilates them directly, they are the truest reality one can think of, and thus they provide the first reference point for linking together the thought processes of which science is made because we receive this either directly through our sensory perceptions or indirectly through accounts from other sources like our teachers, writings, and books. There are no other sources for knowledge.

In physics we have to deal with those experiences that rely on our sensory perceptions of inanimate matter, and such perceptions can then be described in terms of more or less accurate observations and measurements. The content of what we see, hear, and feel directly transforms into unalterable reality. The question is now: With regard to what has already been said, is this frame an adequate basis for physics? Has the task of the physical science been exhaustively identified if one says, this science is meant to make sense out of the content of diversely obtained observations of nature by possibly coming up with an exact, simple, and comprehensive relationship? In order to deal with this question affirmatively, we will consider only the positive aspects of the theory of knowledge as a standpoint that quite a number of renowned physicists and philosophers decidedly support despite the uncertainty that exists these days, and from here on we will name this standpoint "Positivism". Since Auguste Comte, this word was given many different meanings. However, because any further discussion requires clarity, we need to connect this word with a very specific meaning, and the one given is one of the most often used.

To find out whether positivism offers a wide enough basis to support the entire structure of physics, we can think of no better method than to observe where positivism leads us once we are completely convinced that it is the only admissible foundation for physics. Today I want to invite you to try out this method. To begin with, we want to explicitly take up the standpoint of positivism. Thereby, we must obviously make the effort to proceed in a strictly consistent manner, which means that any habitual or instinctive judgments must be excluded. We will however be confronted with some peculiar conclusions, yet we can nevertheless feel assured that logical contradictions cannot happen because we always remain within the sphere of what has been experienced and two experiences can never logically contradict each other. On the other hand, we can rest assured that no experience of any kind will be excluded from our consideration so that we can

4

be absolutely certain that no source of human knowledge is left out.

Therein lies the strength of positivism. It deals with all those questions that can be answered through observations and, inversely, it applies observations to each question in order to come up with an acceptable answer that makes sense. There are no fundamental mysteries in positivism nor are there any unanswered questions left in the dark. Everything is presented in bright daylight.

However, it is not quite that simple to apply positivism comprehensively everywhere to particular cases because our daily language constantly prevents us from doing just that. When we speak about an object like a table for example, we mean something which is different from what is contained in the various observations that we made about the table. We can see the table, touch it, become aware of how solid and hard it is, and if we bump into it we experience some pain, and so on. But, of the thing that exists independently and stands before or behind of all these sensations we know nothing. In the light of positivism, the table is therefore nothing other than a complex correlation of those sensations which we associate with the word table. Virtually nothing remains if we remove all sensations. To ask what a table is "in reality" makes no sense at all and that holds true in general with all physical concepts. The whole world surrounding us is nothing other than the embodiment of experiences in relation to our world. Without them our environment carries no meaning. If a question with regard to the environment is not in one way or another backed up by experience and observation, then that question makes no sense and therefore must be excluded. That is why positivism leaves no room for any kind of metaphysics.

Looking at the sky on a starry night, we see a myriad of images like tiny light points or light disks which actually move in the sky in a way that allows for more or less precise measurements and also allows us to measure their radiation intensity and color. These measurements constitute, from the positivism viewpoint, not only the foundation but also the actual and sole subject matter of astronomy and astrophysics. What we think we understand from such measurements involves human interpretation and imagination. For example, whether we agree with Ptolemy who says: The earth is the stationary center point of the world, and the sun with all the stars move around it; or whether we agree with Copernicus who says: The earth is a tiny insignificant speck of dust in the universe which once a day rotates about its center and once a year turns around the sun. For positivism this is only a different way of formulating observations. These are the only facts. The preference for the Copernican theory depends merely on the way it is expressed. It has proven itself to be simpler and in general more useful to astronomy than the Ptolemaic expressionism that requires many more complications to formulate astronomical laws. Accordingly, Copernicus is not to be appreciated as a ground breaking pioneer but rather as an ingenious inventor.

Due to Copernicus' new world view a radical change pervaded the human mind and a fierce struggle ensued between differing mindsets. However, positivism does not take any more notice of this than it does about the feeling of reverence that the sight of a starry night awakens in a spiritual viewer, when he realizes that every star in the Milky Way is a sun just like our sun and every spiral galaxy is again comparable to the Milky Way whose light takes millions of years to reach us, and that within the immense structure of the universe the earth with the whole human race upon it sinks to an almost incomprehensible insignificance.

Yet, such are thoughts that reach beyond aesthetics and ethics, and since we are dealing only with theoretical questions about the theory of knowledge, we must leave no room at all for such issues to play any role here. Therefore, we will continue to follow our logical train of thoughts.

In accordance with what positivism stands for, since primarily given sensory perceptions are directly connected to reality, therefore it is in principle incorrect to speak about illusions. What can mislead us in some situations are not our sensory perceptions as such but rather the inferences that we draw from them. When we hold a straight stick at an angle in water, we see a bent at the point of immersion whereby the bending we see is not a false impression because it is due to light refraction. Thus, this bending is in fact present as an optical perception. In some cases it is just a different and more useful way of expressing things for some applications if we formulate that our sensory perceptions remain unchanged whether the rod is straight or whether the light rays coming from the submerged end of the rod reach our eyes as being deflected when passing through the water surface.

The essential part of this and of all similar considerations is that viewed from the standpoint of positivism the two ways of expressing things are absolutely, totally, and equally valid. Therefore, there is no point trying to make a choice between them unless, for example, it involves the useful application of the sense of touch as part of a valid decision.

In reality, however, any serious attempt to implement this "as – if" theory may lead to some quite strange and inconvenient consequences. In spite of this, from a logical standpoint the theory remains intact. So let us go on and see where we will finally end up.

Unquestionably, the already mentioned considerations can rightly be applied to animated things in nature. In the light of positivism, a tree, for example, is nothing other than a complex of sensory impressions: We can see that it grows, we can hear the noise from its leaves, and we can breathe in the smell of its flowers. However, when we disregard all of these sensory perceptions then there is virtually nothing left that we may call the "tree as such".

Hence, what is relevant to the world of plants must also be relevant to the world of animals. We may talk about an independent existence or private life of plants and animals simply for reasons of a suggested practicality. One can see that a stepped upon worm is writhing. Yet it makes no sense to ask whether the worm feels pain because only one's own pain can be felt. Therefore, we can only assume that an animal feels pain because this assumption is based on a useful summary of different characteristic side effects in the form of convulsions, contortions, and emitted sounds, the same phenomena that are also triggered in us by our own pain. After talking about animals we may finally talk about people. With regard to positivism, this too requires a clear separation between one's own impressions and those of others because only one's own experiences are real whereas those of others are indirectly developed and, since the experiences of others are in principle something quite different, they must by classified only as purposeful inventions.

Although this perception can be completely implemented without fear of any logical disagreement, this will nevertheless produce a disastrous result that affects the physical science. For if the purpose of physical science is to accomplish no more than to come up with the simplest description of sensory experiences, then it can at the very most deal only with personal experiences because only these are primarily given.

Obviously, even an exceptionally versatile person could not construct a complete science by using his own sensory perceptions and therefore one must choose an alternative. That is, either one gives up any attempt at establishing a fully developed science, although in which case, such a decision would be inconceivable for a radical positivist, or a compromise is made whereby the experiences of others are also admitted as a basis for the science, although in this case the original standpoint, which strictly accepts only what is primary given, must be abandoned since the experiences of others are always

8

secondarily given. Therefore a new factor must be considered, namely, the credibility and reliability of verbal or written reports that are involved in the definition of science. In other words, this factor undermines the original foundation of positivism by logically breaking the chain of scientific evidence which must involve only what is directly given.

This presents a difficulty that we must overcome. Let us assume that all reports about physical experiences are reliable or that we can at least think of an infallible method to eliminate those that are unreliable. With this in mind, it becomes self-evident that all physicists, past and present, that are known to be truthful and thorough should also have the right to claim that their experiences must be acknowledged because it would be unreasonable to exclude them. In particular, it would be totally unwarranted to acknowledge one researcher to a lesser degree simply because other researchers did not have experiences similar to his own.

Viewed from this standpoint it becomes quite difficult to understand and justify why the so called N-rays, which the French physicist René Blondlot discovered in 1903, are completely ignored today although they were investigated in many ways at that time. René Blondlot, as a professor at the University of Nancy, was certainly an excellent and thorough experimenter and his discovery was for him an experience as good as that of any other physicist. We cannot just say that Blondlot became the victim of an illusion because, as we have already seen, illusions are nonexistent in positivistic physics and, therefore, the N-rays can instead be considered as something that was primarily given in reality. Since Blondlot and his institution claimed the discovery of N-rays many years ago no one else has succeeded in reproducing them during all those past years. However, from a positivistic point of view one never knows whether some day under particular circumstances the N-rays may nevertheless become perceptible once again.

One must also take into account that the number of important people whose experiences are of value to the science of physics is in any case quite restricted. Of course, only those personalities who are especially dedicated to science are of importance here since the experiences of others who are not fully involved with science are likely more or less inadequate. Furthermore, to begin with, all theorists are also disqualified since their experiences are essentially limited to using up ink, paper, and brain matter without producing any new material for the development of the science of physics. Thus, only experimental physicists are left, primarily those who have indeed access to exceptionally sensitive instruments, to carry out specific investigations. In fact, only the experiences of a very limited number of people are important to the advancement of physical sciences.

For clarity let us consider three examples: Oersted observed that a galvanic current affected his compass needle, Faraday was first to detect an electromagnetic induction effect, and Hertz used a magnifying glass to look for very tiny electric sparks at the focal point of his parabolic mirror. How can it be understood that these experiments caused such wide spread interest and excitement and brought about such a revolution in the international world of physicists? Nonetheless, this leaves us with an unanswered question, namely, why are the personal experiences of Oersted, Faraday, and Hertz important to physics? For this question positivism can only give a very convoluted and highly unsatisfactory answer. Therefore, positivism must rely on the credibility of a theory that accepts the view that these separate experiences, in themselves insignificant, would lead to a great number of important and successful other experiences of other people, each separate experience increasing the level of credibility of the related experiences. On the other hand, positivism is an excellent theory because it relies on nothing else but a description of given experiences. The question of how it can be acceptable that a particular experience of only one physicist, even rendered with a very primarily given description, becomes relevant for all the other physicists of the whole world, remains uninvestigated. From the standpoint of positivism such a question must be rejected because it is of no use to investigate something which is physically meaningless.

It is easy to see the reason for this unusual way of looking at things. When carried out consistently, positivism denies the concept and necessity of an objectively independent physics, in other words, physics depends on the individuality of researchers. In this regard, positivism must remain consistent because it absolutely accepts no other reality than the experiments of individual physicists. In light of this summary, I no longer need to ask myself whether positivism is adequate enough for the foundation of the science of physics because that question has been unambiguously answered. Thus, a science that in principle deprives itself of objectivity must rely on its own judgment. The basis that positivism provides for physics is firmly founded but it is too narrow. Something sufficiently meaningful must be added to enlarge the basis, which is the idea that science should be freed as much as possible from the contingencies brought into it by reference to specific human individuals. This cannot be done through formal logic. Instead, this must mainly be done hypothetically by applying reasonable metaphysical concepts. That entails that our experiences by themselves cannot tell us very much about the actual physical world, they merely bear witness to the existence of another world that stands, independent from us, behind them, in other words, a real external world.

In that case, we can do away with the positivistic expression "as – if" and we can apply to the so called useful inventions, of which we have already presented some specific examples, an appropriately higher level of reality. This implies that the direct descriptions of the indirect sensory impressions exist in reality. This shifts the task of physics from focusing on experiences to now endeavor to understand the real external world.

However, we must now deal with a new epistemological problem because positivism quite rightly insists that sensory perceptions are the only source of knowledge. The two sentences "there is a real external world that exists independently from us" and "the real external world is not directly recognizable" when taken together form a crucial center point for the entire science of physics. These two sentences stand in opposition to each other and by that open up a path to irrationality. This situation adheres not only to physics but to every other science as well. In other words, science can never completely explain everything. We must accept this as a fact that cannot be changed. That is, we cannot, as in positivism, remove facts from the world by suitably limiting the work of science. In that way the work of science can only be seen as an endless endeavor to reach a goal that we cannot and never will reach. In that case the goal as such will inherently be metaphysical by standing behind every experience.

Does that not proclaim that every science is meaningless and is only a wild goose chase? Not at all, because we can accumulate the fruits of our labor in order to assemble a growing pool of knowledge that will unveil some tangible evidence of reality which leads us to proceed in the right direction. In this way we can get closer and closer to the unreachable goal that always remains at a distance. It is not the possession of truth but rather the successful search for it that stimulates and pleases a researcher. Insightful thinkers have known this for a long time before Lessing gave it its present classical interpretation.

II

For a Physicist the ideal goal is to attain knowledge of the real external world, however, he will not succeed to reach that goal through measurements as the only available research tool. In other words, measurements are never directly relevant to the real world. They only provide more or less uncertain messages of information. Or, as Helmholtz once formulated, measurements are a signal that the real world sends from which he can draw conclusions in a way similar to that of a linguist puzzling out a document that originated from a culture totally unfamiliar to him. For his work to possibly be successful, with reference to Helmholtz's remark, he must assume that the document refers to something that reasonably makes sense. In the same way a physicist must always presuppose that the real world complies with certain understandable laws, even if he has no expectation of completely understanding these laws nor that he could predetermine their nature with certainty in advance.

By trusting in the law-abiding nature of the real world, a physicist can establish a so called physical worldview through a system of concepts and sentences which, to the best of his knowledge and ability, not only represent the real world but also sends him, if possible, the same messages as the real world. Provided he succeeds in this he can certainly assert without worrying about any factual objection that he has truly unveiled a new side of the real world, although it will never be possible to directly prove such a revelation. Without appearing arrogant, one may express one's amazement and admiration of the high level of perfection of the human searching mind which since the time of Aristotle shaped our physical worldview. Looking at this from the standpoint of positivism, the idea of a physical worldview and the continual struggle for knowledge acquisition about reality would, of course, seem rather strange and senseless since without an available object to consider, nothing exists to be described.

The task of the physical worldview can be characterized by saying that it must establish as close a connection as possible between the real world and the world of sensory experiences. It is the latter which supplies the material to start with, but the processing of the material actually proceeds by separating and removing from the complex of physical experience as many items as possible that might be caused by the peculiarities of our five sense organs and of the measuring devices being used.

For the rest, the physical worldview has to fulfil only one more condition to start with, namely, that it remains altogether logically consistent. Apart from that any creative agent has complete freedom, he can use his unlimited autonomy and does not have to worry about the power of his imagination. Of course, this can introduce a significant amount of arbitrariness and uncertainty which will convert the nature of the task into something much more complicated than what a first glance a candid scrutiny can reveal. Already the first step, namely the assembly of all the individually measured results into a single law, must involve free speculation since the researcher must all at once inspect the resulting individual measurements and somehow decide what to do with them. In other words, the task he faces is like placing a great number of dots on paper in order to connect them by a single curve. However, no matter how close the dots are placed, we can nonetheless connect them by an endless number of curves of the same type. Even if one uses a continuously moving recording device which can draw a complete curve autonomously, like a temperature curve for example. The curve thus produced will never resemble a sharp and narrow curve but will look like a more or less broad curve which can accommodate an endless number of the narrow type within itself.

There are no generally useful rules for leaving uncertainty behind and instead come to a certain decision. The solution of this apparent problem requires the introduction of a hypothesis resulting from certain specific interconnections between ideas that encourage us to form in advance a certain idea about what specific curve that we should select as the most suitable and exact among an endless number of curves.

The origin of such a new hypothesis lies beyond all logic. In order to come to terms with this, a physicist must possess two attributes, expertise and creative imagination. This is conditional in two ways: First, a physicist must excel in performing all kinds of accurate measurements and secondly, he must come up with an idea that will show that two different types of measuring experiments have something in common. Every powerful hypothesis depends on a likely combination of two different types of experiments.

To highlight this we can look at several historical examples: – Archimedes compared the weight loss of his body in water with the weight loss of the gold crown of the Tyrant of Syracuse dipped in water. – Newton supposedly compared the fall of an apple from a tree with the movement of the moon with respect to the earth. – Einstein compared the state of a gravitating body inside a box at rest with the state of a gravity-free body inside an upwards accelerating box. And, – Bohr compared the orbiting of an electron around the atomic nucleus with the orbiting of a planet around the sun. It would indeed be interesting to find out how great a number of meaningful hypotheses of physics originate through the comparison of ideas. However, it would be quite difficult to actually carry out such a task. Very often, for some personal reasons, expert creators of new ideas do not like to expose their well thought out hypotheses to the public, since these frequently also contain something irrelevant.

The usefulness of any hypothesis depends on the consequences which one can derive from it. This has to be done logically in a mathematical manner by using the hypothesis as a starting point in order to develop as complete a theory as possible. By connecting specific statements of the theory with measurements one can determine whether such a connection is adequate or not, in other words, whether one can draw favorable or unfavorable conclusions from the initial hypothesis.

In this case a remarkable fact reveals itself namely, that progress in physics does not happen at a steady advance by gradually improving and refining our knowledge but rather happens from time to time in an explosive manner. Every new hypothesis that appears looks at first glance like a sudden eruption, like a jump into the unknown, or like something that defies any logical explanation. But once the new hypothesis gives birth to a new theory things start to change. In other words, once the new theory has seen the light of day it will steadily keep evolving until it finally meets its fate through measurements. The longer the theory's fate turns out favorable the more and more its initial hypothesis gains prestige and as a consequence, the further development of the theory happens in ever widening circles. However, as soon as difficulties are encountered with the measurements, doubt, mistrust, and critical feelings arise. This signals the withering of the old hypothesis and the maturation of a new hypothesis which must resolve this crisis by a new theory as an improvement over the old one. Thus the advancement of knowledge in physics depends, to a lesser or greater degree, on the continuous interplay of theories in order to explore the real external world, sometimes on a small scale, sometimes on a large scale and the history of physics exemplifies this interplay. Whoever follows in detail, via continuous measurements, the development of the splendid Lorentz theory of the electrodynamic of moving bodies will understand the difficulties and conflicts that were involved. When the hypothesis of relativity finally became established it brought about a feeling of relief. Something similar can be observed with regard to the quantum hypothesis except that it has not as yet completely resolved its crisis.

Only the creator of a hypothesis decides its terminology, he is free to use any terms and sentences and string them together in any which way provided that they do not show any logical contradiction. In that way the creator maintains complete sovereignty over his hypothesis. Amongst physicist some claim that to establish a sufficiently justified hypothesis of physics one must only admit such terms whose meaning is sufficiently defined through measurements to begin with, in other words, independently of any theory. This assumption is false in two ways: First, every hypothesis belonging to the worldview of physics is a product of the freely speculating human mind and second, a physical dimension that can be measured independently does not really exist. Instead, the physical meaning of a measurement depends entirely on the interpretation that a theory gives it. Anyone who worked at a well equipped research laboratory can confirm that even the most direct and precise measurement, with respect to gravity or testing the intensity of an electrical current for example, still necessitates many corrections in order to be of any use in physics. However, the necessary corrections can only be derived from a theory and therefore from a hypothesis.

Thus, the creator of a hypothesis has almost unlimited possibilities and resources which he can use without having to rely very much on the services of his physiological sense organs or physical measuring devices. It is by means of his mind's eye of that a creator observes and inspects the finest processes that take place in physical structures: He closely monitors the motion of every electron, he knows the frequency and phase of every wave, and he even freely creates his own geometry to describe his rational endeavors. That is to say, that with his mental tools, which are his instruments of ideal precision, the creator of a hypothesis can freely investigate anyone of many physical events in order to perform the most adventurous thought experiments from which he can draw far-ranging conclusions. Of course, such conclusions have nothing to do with real measurements. Hence it is impossible to directly prove through measurements whether a hypothesis as such is true or false. The only thing that can be shown is whether a hypothesis is more or less useful.

And this brings us to the flip side of the coin. The ideal clairvoyance of the mind's eye, with regard to all naturally occurring processes in the physical world, only comes about because this world is only a self made mental image of the real world. Thus, the perfect knowledge of it through this limitlessly powerful insight of the mind's eye becomes fundamentally self evident. For every hypothesis in physics, the reality of the world becomes fundamentally self-evident. Every hypothesis in physics attains its meaning with respect to physical reality and its actual value only if the theory based on it is related to measuring experiments. But, we have already seen that an indirect measurement tells us just as little about the physical worldview as about the real world. Rather, every measurement relates to a certain process which involves the physicist's sense organs and the measuring device he uses. From this we can only say for certain that the physicist is somehow connected to the real event being measured. This means that in a physical sense a measurement is not directly given and therefore, the evaluation of a measurement is as much a task of science as the investigation of the logical unfolding of any other process. Consequently, research uses the same method as science, namely, all the details of the measuring process must be placed within the physical worldview. Therefore, one must try to see through the sense organs of the measuring physicist as well as his measuring device and of the processes taking place in them with the ideally clairvoyant mind's eye. In this way only is it possible to explore the correlation between the measuring experiences and the nature of the measured event. With regard to theoretical knowledge, difficulties in theoretical physics recently arose through the development of the quantum hypothesis. Apparently these difficulties seem to be due to the fact that, in an unjustified manner, the biological eye of the measuring physicist has become identified with the mind's eye of the speculating physicist, although the former is the object of the latter.

Since every measurement involves to a lesser or greater degree a noticeable causal intervention in the measuring process, it is generally impossible to disconnect the laws defining the progress of the physical events from the methods by which they are measured, although for more complex processes, like those that involve many atoms, it does not really matter which methods are used to take measurements. Previously, during the so called classical period, theoretical physics gradually embraced the assumption that measurements allow us to directly look at real physical events. We already know from our discussion that this assumption is in principle false. It is false due to the inherent mistake of positivism to consider only the measuring experiments and completely ignore the real processes. It is not permissible nor is it possible to completely ignore measurements and to directly consider instead the real processes. Now, we have a quantum theory which entails a numerical constant that determines precisely and indivisibly the limit of any quantum activity and nothing can supersede this quantum limit. That is to say, that no matter how precise physical measurements are performed, the methods used cannot provide answers to all the questions about the very small details of real events. This leads to the conclusion that such questions do not make any physical sense at all. At this point, we must submit the results of measurements to free speculation in order to round out the physical worldview as well as possible so that we can gain a more profound insight of the real world.

When we look back we can say that the progress in physics in terms of content depends to begin with upon the development of measuring methods. In that respect we share the standpoint of positivism. However, our point of view differs from that of positivism. According to positivism experimental measurements constitute the primary and indivisible elements upon which every science depends. In contrast to this view, real measurements in physics are regarded as the more or less intricate end result of interaction between the processes in the outside world and the processes in the measuring instruments or sensory organs, the proper disentanglement of which being a major task of scientific research. Therefore, first of all, the measurements must be arranged in an appropriate order because every test arrangement defines the specific formulation of a particular question to nature.

Nonetheless, one cannot formulate a reasonable question without the help of a reasonable theory. In other words, for a question or judgment to make sense in physics, one must not rely on what one believes but rather rely on a well founded theory. It is often the case that a certain question in physics makes sense according to one theory but does not make sense according to another theory. Thus the specifics of a question must stand in relation to the significance of a theory.

For example, let us consider the question of how to change the non-noble metal mercury into gold. This question seriously made sense during the times of the alchemists. A countless number of researcher lost their wealth and health in trying to solve this puzzle. However, once the teaching about the unchanging nature of atoms became established, the question no longer made sense and people who still pursued it were called foolish. Today, since the introduction of the Bohr atomic model whereby the gold atom differs from the mercury atom by the loss of a single electron, this puzzling question gained consideration once again and the most modern research resources are used to solve it. This shows that as a last resort trying beats studying since even an unsuccessful attempt, if correctly interpreted, delivers some important knowledge.

Thus, the more or less random experiments carried out to produce gold unexpectedly contributed to the advancement of science: The scientific foundation of chemistry evolved. From the unsolvable problem of perpetual motion arose the principle of conservation of energy. An unsuccessful attempt was made to measure the absolute motion of the earth. And the theory of relativity was published. Experimental and theoretical research depends on each other and neither can advance without the other.

Admittedly, it is sometimes tempting once a new insight has been gained, not only to declare afterwards that certain related problems are pointless, but also to want to prove their futility a priori. But this is an illusion. In itself, the absolute motion of the earth, that is, the motion of the earth with respect to the luminiferous aether, and the absolute Newtonian space are not physically meaningless, as can be read in some popular representations of the theory of relativity. The former becomes so only when special relativity is introduced, the latter when general relativity is introduced.

From what has been seen so far, we can observe that certain scientific views that have survived for hundreds of years are waved and ultimately replaced by new and more powerful scientific theories.

III

Even in light of the scientifically established foundation of all the natural sciences, which is the law of causality, opinions about the law of causality are still divided. This raises three questions: Does the assumption that this law of causality applies to every physical event hold true, and is this law robustly applicable to all particular cases like the smallest events in atoms? Or, does this law have only a numerical and statistical meaning when applied to the finest processes in atoms? This issue cannot be answered from the outset, neither epistemologically nor can such issues be resolved through measurements. However, to begin with, it depends on the discretion of the speculating and hypothesizing physicist whether he prefers to apply causality from a standpoint of strict dynamics or statistics. What is crucial here is how far a physicist can go with this. One can check this out in the following manner. To start with, to investigate things one must select one of the two standpoints in order to arrive at some tentative results to look at. After that we can proceed with the investigation in the same manner by which we investigated the achievements of positivism today at the beginning of our discussion. In principle it does not matter which standpoint is selected first. However, for practical reasons, one should start with the one that looks the most promising to produce satisfactory results. On my part, I positively believe that the choice of a robust causality is preferable because the dynamics of a naturally unfolding law reaches out farther and deeper than the statistical approach, which to begin with, renounces certain values of knowledge.

Statistical physics only deals with natural laws that involve a plurality of events. Although single events are statistically introduced and accepted, the question of their logical trajectory is at once declared senseless. It seems to me that such a situation is highly unsatisfactory. Up to now I do not see the slightest reason that would force me to give up the important dynamics of the law of nature by which every change in nature is produced by some cause, neither in a physical, nor in the intellectual world view.

However, a causally supported natural law is not directly applicable to a succession of experiences. One can always interconnect experiences in a statistical manner and even the most accurate measurements may occasionally contain some unavoidable mistakes. Nonetheless, in an objective sense, any experience involves a process by which many diverse elements are produced. Therefore, any single element stands in a one on one causal relation with another single element of another closely following experience. Although it depends on the type of experience to be considered as well as upon the results that can possibly be accomplished, experience as such can nonetheless be regarded as the cause by which diverse experiences are interconnected, depending on the nature of its elementary composition.

With regard to our rigorous precondition of causality we arrived at a seemingly insurmountable barrier which we must overcome intellectually and, since this barrier concerns all of us, I would now like to address the important issue of free will. For freedom of will is directly guaranteed to us by our awareness as the last and highest instance of our cognitive capacity.

Is the human will truly free or is it causally predetermined? These two alternatives seem to be completely mutually exclusive. But, since the first alternative must obviously be answered positively, it seems that, by adopting a strict causality in one case, the other alternative must be taken *ad absurdum*.

Many attempts have been made to resolve this dilemma. This was often done in such a manner whereby a limit was established beyond which the validity of the law of causality could not reach. Recently, this way of thinking affected the modern evolution of physics, whereby modern developments in physics are used to support the assumption that only statistical causality accounts for everything. As I already occasionally indicated, I am unable to agree with such an assumption. If this assumption were correct, human free will would be nothing more than a blind instrument of blind chance. In my opinion the question about free will has nothing to do with the difference between causal or statistical physics because the meaning of free will applies much deeper than that since free will is completely independent of any physical or biological hypothesis.

I believe, in general agreement with renowned philosophers that the solution of this two sided dilemma lies in a completely different direction. Upon closer examination, the already presented alternative of whether the human will is free or is strictly causally determined, relies on a logically inadmissible disjunction. These two opposed cases actually are not at all mutually exclusive. What does it actually mean to say that human will is causally determined? This can only make sense if every human action, together with all that motivates it, can be foreseen and predetermined and that, of course, can only be done by someone who is completely aware of the experience of another person. In other words, his absolute awareness must encompass all of the physical and mental features as well as the conscious and unconscious states of the other person. And for that, moreover, he must possess the supreme clairvoyance of the mind's eye, or can we say that he must possess a godlike eye. To that we can and must agree without contradiction. Before God, all human beings even the most perfect and genial ones like Goethe or Mozart are primitive creatures whose most secret thoughts and most subtle emotions are like pearls on a string whereby each pearl follows another in a regular sequence. This does not allow for any credit to the worthiness of great men. One must always keep in mind that under these considerations any attempt to imitate the godly eye would be presumptuous and senseless since we can never completely understand the thoughts of such a divine intellect. The ordinary human intellect would never be able to understand such deepest thoughts even if they would be directly communicated. In that regard, a proposition of the determinacy of intellectual processes in many cases eludes any examination because the proposition is metaphysical in nature and the same holds for the proposition that there is a real external world. However, it is logically irrefutable that such a proposition carries an important meaning. Proof of this lies with the simple fact that it is the basis of all scientific research about the connections between mental processes. No biographer will leave the question of the motivation of a remarkable action of his hero to coincidence. Most likely he will always find the lack of a satisfactory explanation to be due to the incompleteness of the source materials given or, if he is insightful enough, with the limits of his own power of comprehension. This applies to our practical life as well, we adjust our behavior with other people always under the assumption that their words and actions are due to quite specific causes that are determined through either every person's inherent nature or through the outside environment, even if these causes are often not recognizable by us.

What does it mean when we say on the other hand: The human will is free! It only means that any person who faces two possibilities for action can choose one or the other at his own discretion. This does not at all present a contradiction but rather stands up as a summary of what has already been said. It would present a contradiction only if a case could be made whereby a person could completely look at himself with a godlike eye. In that case, on the basis of the law of causality, he could foresee his own volitional actions and his will would no longer be free. However, this case is already excluded for purely logical reasons. Even the most sensitive eye is no more able to look at itself than any tool can work on itself. Object and subject of any cognitive activity can never be identical because one can talk about cognition only if the object to be recognized is not influenced by the processes of the subject. Therefore it makes no sense at all to ask whether the validity of the law of causality can be applied to the volitional actions of any person, just as it makes no sense at all to ask whether a person can climb above himself by himself or whether he can compete in a race with his own shadow.

However, generally anybody can apply the law of causality to the physical or mental processes in his environment according to the extent of his own intelligence, provided that this application has no influence upon his present and future thoughts and cognitive activities.

Together they are the only object that eludes the constraints of the law of causality and, in this way, this object is the most precious and very personal possession on which the peace and happiness of every one of us depends. The law of causality offers no help in leading everyone's actions in the right direction, nor can it release anyone from his moral obligations. The issue of morality has nothing to do with the law of causality, but pertains to a very different law, that relates to our conscience, which is clearly enough recognizable if one wishes to understand oneself.

It is a dangerous self-delusion if one tries to escape from an inconvenient moral law and instead call upon an inevitable natural law. A human being who looks upon his future as inevitably determined by fate or a people who believes in prophecies by which their demise is determined by the law of nature, in reality only indicate that they lack the proper will to ascend above all that.

Ladies and Gentlemen! We arrived at a point here at which science as such must acknowledge and declare that any further considerations belong to fields far beyond its own application. The fact that science is able to apply this kind of self-denial should, in my opinion, strongly encourage us to trust the reliability of the results which have been achieved in its own field. Nonetheless we can also observe that the different fields in which the human mind is active are not completely separated from each other but are rather most intimately related. We started with a single specialized science which by raising questions of a purely physical type led us beyond the sensory world into the real metaphysical world. Although it seems impossible to directly understand the real metaphysical world, it confronts us as something mysterious and incomprehensibly sublime, while at the same time, in our attempts to depict it, we can sense some profound internal harmony and beauty.

We can now say that we have addressed the most prevalent questions which must be of concern to anybody who wants at least once to think seriously about the meaning of his life. I hope that those of you who are not very familiar with physics have nevertheless gained the impression that a specialized science, if carried out thoroughly and conscientiously, can just as well unveil valuable treasures of aesthetical and ethical nature. And furthermore with regard to the great intellectual crises of which we spoke at the beginning of our discussion, and upon which we based our follow up considerations, ultimately they only serve as a last instance to prepare a consolidation towards a new greater unity.

2 Positivism and Realism

by Moritz Schlick

Published in *Erkenntnis*, Volume 3 (1932), pp. 1-31. Translated into English by Peter Heath and published in Moritz Schlick, *Philosophical Papers*, Volume II (1925-1936), edited by Henk L. Mulder Mulder and B.F.B. van de Velde-Schlick (D. Reidel Publishing Company, Dordrecht 1979), pp. 259-284.

I. Preliminary Questions

Every philosophical movement is defined by the principles that it regards as fundamental, and to which it constantly recurs in its arguments. But in the course of historical development, the principles are apt not to remain unaltered, whether it be that they acquire new formulations, and come to be extended or restricted, or that even their meaning gradually undergoes noticeable modifications. At some point the question then arises as to whether we should still speak at all of the development of a single movement and retain its old name, or whether a new movement has not in fact arisen.

If, alongside the evolved outlook, an 'orthodox' movement still continues to exist, which clings to the first principles in their original form and meaning, then sooner or later some terminological distinction of the old from the new will automatically come about. But where this is not clearly so, and where, on the contrary, the most diverse and perhaps contradictory formulations and interpretations of the principles are bandied about among the various adherents of a 'movement', then a hubbub arises, whose result is that supporters and opponents of the view are found talking at cross purposes; every one seeks out from the principles what he can specifically use for the defense of his own view, and everything ends in hopeless misunderstandings and obscurities. They only disappear when the various principles are separated from each other and tested individually for meaning and truth on their own account, in which process we do best, at first, to disregard entirely the contexts in which they have historically arisen, and the names that have been given to them.

I should like to apply these considerations to the modes of thought grouped under the name of 'positivism'. From the moment when Auguste Comte invented the term, up to the present day, they have undergone a development which provides a good-example of what has just been said. I do this, however, not with the historical purpose of establishing, say, a rigorous concept of positivism in its historical manifestation, but rather in order to contribute to a real settlement of the controversy currently carried on about certain principles which rank as positivist axioms. Such a settlement is all the dearer to me, in that I subscribe to some of these principles myself. My only concern here is to make the meaning of these principles as clear as possible; whether, after such clarification people are still minded to impute them to 'positivism' or not, is a question of wholly subordinate importance.

If every view is to be labelled positivist, which denies the possibility of metaphysics, then nothing can be said against it as a mere definition, and in *this* sense I would have to declare myself a strict positivist. But this, of course, is true only if we presuppose a particular definition of 'metaphysics'. What the definition of metaphysics is, that would have to be made basic here, does not need to interest us at present; but it scarcely accords with the formulations that are mostly current in the literature of philosophy; and closer definitions of positivism that adhere to such formulations lead straight into obscurities and difficulties.

For if, say — as has mostly been done from time immemorial — we assert that metaphysics is the doctrine of 'true being', of 'reality in itself, or of 'transcendent being', this talk of true, real being obviously presupposes that a non-true, lesser or apparent being stands opposed to it, as has indeed been assumed by all metaphysicians since the days of Plato and the Eleatics. This seeming being is said to be the realm of 'appearances', and while the true transcendent reality is held to be accessible with difficulty only to the efforts of the metaphysician, the special sciences are exclusively concerned with appearances, and the latter are also perfectly accessible to scientific knowledge. The contrast in the knowability of the two 'kinds of being' is then traced to the fact that appearances are 'given' and immediately known to us, whereas metaphysical reality has had to be inferred from them only by a circuitous route. With this we seem to have arrived at a fundamental concept of the positivists, for they, too, are always talking of the 'given', and state their basic principle mostly by saying that, like the scientist, the philosopher must abide throughout in the given, that an advance beyond it, such as the metaphysician attempts, is impossible or absurd.

It is natural, therefore, to take the given of positivism to be simply identical with the metaphysician's appearances, and to believe that positivism is at bottom a metaphysics from which the transcendent has been omitted or struck out; and such a view may often enough have inspired the arguments of positivists, no less than those of their adversaries. But with this we are already on the road to dangerous errors.

This very term 'the given' is already an occasion for grave misunderstandings. 'To give', of course, normally signifies a three-termed relation: it presupposes in the first place someone who gives, secondly someone given to, and thirdly something given. For the metaphysician this is quite in order, for the giver is transcendent reality, the receiver is the knowing consciousness, and the latter appropriates what is given to it as its 'content'. But the positivist, from the outset, will obviously have nothing to do with such notions; the given, for him, is to be merely a term for what is simplest and no longer open to question. Whatever term we may choose, indeed, it will be liable to occasion misconceptions; if we talk of 'acquaintance' ['Erlebnis'], we seem to presuppose the distinction between he who is acquainted and what he is acquainted with; in employing the term 'content of consciousness', we appear to burden ourselves with a similar distinction, and also with the complex concept of 'consciousness', first ex- cogitated, at all events, by philosophical thought.

But even apart from such difficulties, it is possibly still not yet clear what is actually meant by the given. Does it merely include such 'qualities' as 'blue', 'hot' and 'pain', or also, for example, relations between them, or the order they are in? Is the similarity of two qualities 'given' in the same sense as the qualities themselves? And if the given is somehow elaborated or interpreted or judged, is this elaboration or judgement not also in turn a given in some sense?

It is not obscurities of this type, however, which give occasion to present-day controversies; it is the question of 'reality' that first tosses among the parties the apple of discord.

If positivism's rejection of metaphysics amounts to a denial of transcendent reality, it seems the most natural thing in the world to conclude that in that case it attributes reality only to non-transcendent being. The main principle of the positivist then seems to run: 'Only the given is real'. Anyone who takes pleasure in plays upon words could even make use of a peculiarity of the German language in order to lend this proposition the air of being a self-evident tautology, by formulating it as: *'Es gibt nur das Gegebene'* [Only the given exists].

What are we to say of this principle?

Many positivists may have stated and upheld it (particularly those, perhaps, who have treated physical objects as 'mere logical constructions' or as 'mere auxiliary concepts'), and others have had it imputed to them by opponents — but we are obliged to say that anyone who asserts this principle thereby attempts to advance a claim that is metaphysical in the same sense, and to the same degree, as the seemingly opposite contention, that 'There is a transcendent reality'.

The problem at issue here is obviously the so-called question as to the reality of the external world and on this there seem to be two parties: that of 'realism', which believes in the reality of the external world, and that of 'positivism', which does not believe in this. I am convinced that in fact it is quite absurd to set two views in contrast to one another in this fashion, since (as with all metaphysical propositions) both parties, at bottom, have not the least notion of what they are trying to say. But before explaining this I should like to show how the most natural interpretations of the proposition 'only the given is real' in fact lead at once to familiar metaphysical views.

As a question about the existence of the 'external' world, the problem can make its appearance only through drawing a distinction of some kind between inner and outer, and this happens inasmuch and insofar as the given is regarded as a 'content' of consciousness, as belonging to a subject (or several) to *whom* it is given. The immediate data are thereby credited with a conscious character, the character of presentations or ideas; and the proposition in question would then assert that *all* reality possesses this character: no being outside consciousness. But this is nothing else but the basic principle of metaphysical *idealism*. If the philosopher thinks he can speak only of what is given to himself, we are confronted with a solipsistic metaphysics; but if he thinks he may assume that the given is distributed to many subjects, we then have an idealism of the Berkeleyan type.

On this interpretation, positivism would thus be simply identical with the older idealist metaphysics. But since its founders were certainly seeking something quite other than a renewal of that idealism, this view must be rejected as inconsistent with the antimetaphysical purpose of positivism. Idealism and positivism do not go together, The positivist Ernst Laas (1) devoted a work in several volumes to demonstrating the irreconcilable opposition that exists between them in all areas; and if his pupil Hans Vaihinger gave his *Philosophy of As If* the subtitle of an 'idealist positivism', that is just one of the contradictions that infect this work. Ernst Mach has particularly emphasized that his own positivism has evolved in a direction away from the Berkeleyan metaphysics; he and Avenarius laid much stress on not construing the given as a content of consciousness, and endeavored to keep this notion out of their philosophy altogether.

In view of the uncertainty in the positivists' own camp, it is not surprising if the 'realist' ignores the distinctions we have mentioned and directs his arguments against the thesis that 'there are only contents of consciousness', or that 'there is only an internal world'. But this proposition belongs to the idealist metaphysics; it has no place in an antimetaphysical positivism, and these counter-arguments do not tell against such a view.

The 'realist' can, indeed, take the line that it is utterly inevitable that the given should be regarded as a content of consciousness, as subjective, or mental — or whatever the term may be; and he would consider the attempts of Avenarius and Mach to construe the given as neutral and to do away with the inner-outer distinction, as a failure, and would think a theory without metaphysics to be simply impossible. But this line of argument is more rarely encountered. And whatever the position there, we are dealing in any case with a quarrel about nothing, since the 'problem of the reality of the external world' is a meaningless pseudo-problem. It is now time to make this clear.

II. On the Meaning of Statements

It is the proper business of philosophy to seek for and clarify the *meaning* of claims and questions. The chaotic state in which philosophy has found itself throughout the greatest part of its history is traceable to the unlucky fact that firstly it has accepted certain formulations with far too much naivete, as genuine problems, without first carefully testing whether they really possessed a sound meaning; and secondly, that it has believed the answers to certain questions to be discoverable by particular philosophical methods that differ from those of the special sciences. By philosophical analysis we are unable to decide of anything whether it is real; we can only determine what it *means* to claim that it is real; and whether this is then the case or not can only be decided by the ordinary methods of daily life and science, namely by *experience*. So here the task is to get clear whether a meaning can be attached to the question about the reality of the 'external world'.

When are we certain, in general that the meaning of a question is clear to us? Obviously then, and only then, when we are in a position to state quite accurately the circumstances under which it can be answered in the affirmative — or those under which it would have to receive a negative answer. By these statements, and these alone, is the meaning of the question defined.

It is the first step in every kind of philosophizing, and the basis of all reflection, to realize that it is absolutely impossible to give the meaning of any claim save by describing the state-of-affairs that must obtain if the claim is to be true. If it does not obtain, then the claim is false. The meaning of a proposition obviously consists in this alone, that it expresses a particular state-of-affairs. This state-of-affairs must actually be pointed out, in order to give the meaning of the proposition. One may say, indeed, that the proposition itself already gives this state-of-affairs; but only, of course, for one who *understands* it. But when do I understand a proposition? When I know the meaning of the words that occur in it? This can be explained by definitions. But in the definitions new words occur, whose meaning I also have to know in turn. The business of defining cannot go on indefinitely, so eventually we come to words whose meaning cannot again be described in a proposition; it has to be pointed out directly; the meaning of the word must ultimately be *shown*, it has to be *given*. This takes place through an act of pointing or showing, and what is shown must be given, since otherwise it cannot be pointed out to me.

In order, therefore, to find the meaning of a proposition, we have to transform it by introduction of successive definitions, until finally only such words appear in it as can no longer be defined, but whose meanings can only be indicated directly. The criterion for the truth or falsity of the proposition then consists in this, that under specific conditions (stated in the definitions) certain data are, or are not, present. Once this is established, I have established everything that the proposition was talking about, and hence I know its meaning. If I am *not* capable, in principle, of verifying a proposition, that is, if I have absolutely no knowledge of how I should go about it, what I would have to do, in order to ascertain its truth or falsity, then I obviously have no idea at all of what the proposition is actually saying; for then I would be in no position to interpret the proposition, in proceeding, by means of the definitions, from its wording to possible data, since insofar as I *am* in a position to do this, I can also, by this very fact, point out the road to verification in principle (even though, for practical reasons, I may often be unable actually to tread it). To state the circumstances under which a proposition is true is the *same* as stating its meaning, and nothing else.

And these 'circumstances', as we have now seen, have ultimately to be found in the given. Different circumstances imply differences in the given. The *meaning* of every proposition is ultimately determined by the given alone, and by absolutely nothing else.

I do not know if this view should be described as positivistic; though I should like to believe that it has been in the background of all efforts that go under this name in the history of philosophy, whether, indeed, it has been clearly formulated or not. It may well be assumed to constitute the true core and driving force of many quite erroneous formulations that we find among the positivists.

Anyone who has once attained the insight, that the meaning of any statement can be determined only by the given, no longer even grasps the *possibility of another* opinion, for he sees that he has merely discerned the conditions under which opinions can be formulated at all. It would thus be quite erroneous as well to perceive in the foregoing any sort of 'theory of meaning' (in Anglo-Saxon countries the view outlined, that the meaning of a statement is wholly and solely determined by its verification in the given, is commonly called the 'experimental theory of meaning'); that which precedes all formation of theories cannot itself be a theory.

The content of our thesis is in fact entirely trivial (and that is precisely why it can give so much insight); it tells us that a statement only has a specifiable meaning if it makes some testable difference whether it is true or false. A proposition for which the World looks exactly the same when it is true as it does when it is false, in fact says nothing whatever about the world; it is empty, it conveys nothing, I can specify no meaning for it. But a *testable* difference is present only if there is a difference in the given, for to be testable certainly means nothing else but 'demonstrable in the given'.

It is self-evident that the term 'testability' is intended only *in principle*, for the meaning of a proposition does not, of course, depend on whether the circumstances under which we actually find ourselves at a given moment allow of, or prevent actual verification. The statement that 'there are 10,000 ft mountains on the far side of the moon' is beyond doubt absolutely meaningful, although we lack the technical means for verifying it. And it would remain just as meaningful even if we knew for certain, on scientific grounds of some kind, that no man would ever reach the far side of the moon. Verification always remains *thinkable*, we are always able to say what sort of data we should have to encounter, in order to effect the decision; it is *logically* possible, whatever the situation may be as regards the actual possibility of doing it. And that is all that is at issue here.

But if someone advanced the claim, that within every electron there is a nucleus which is always present, but produces absolutely no effects outside, so that its existence in nature is discernible in no way whatever — then this would be a meaningless claim. For we should at once have to ask the fabricator of this hypothesis: What, then, do you actually *mean* by the presence of this 'nucleus'?, and he could only reply: I mean that something exists there in the electron. We would then go on to ask: What is that supposed to mean? How would it be if this something did not exist? And he would have to reply: In that case, everything else would be exactly as before. For according to his claim, no effects of any kind proceed from this something, and everything observable would remain absolutely unaltered, the realm of the given would not be touched. We would judge that he had not succeeded in conveying to us the meaning of his hypothesis, and that it is therefore vacuous. In this case the impossibility of verification is actually not a factual, but a *logical* impossibility, since the claim that this nucleus is totally without effects rules out, *in principle*, the possibility of deciding by differences in the given.

Nor can it be supposed that the distinction between essential impossibility of verification and a merely factual and

38

empirical impossibility is not sharp, and therefore often hard to draw; for the 'essential' impossibility is simply a logical one, which differs from the empirical not by degrees, but absolutely. What is merely empirically impossible still remains *thinkable*; but what is logically impossible is contradictory, and cannot, therefore, be thought at all. We also find, in fact, that with sure instinct, this distinction is always very clearly sensed in the practice of scientific thinking. The physicists would be the first to reject the claim in our example, concerning the eternally hidden nucleus of the electron, with the criticism that this is no hypothesis whatever, but an empty play with words. And on the question of the meaning of their statements, successful students of reality have at all times adopted the standpoint here outlined, in that they acted upon it, even though mostly unawares.

Thus our position does not represent anything strange and peculiar for science, but in a certain sense has always been a self-evident thing. It could not possibly have been otherwise, because only from this standpoint can the truth of a statement be tested at all; since all scientific activity consists in testing the truth of statements, it constantly acknowledges the correctness of our viewpoint by what it does.

If express confirmation be still needed, it is to be found with the utmost clarity at critical points in the development of science, where research is compelled to bring its self-evident presuppositions to consciousness. This situation occurs where difficulties of principle give rise to the suspicion that something may not be in order about these presuppositions. The most celebrated example of this kind, which will forever remain notable, is Einstein's analysis of the concept of time, which consists in nothing else whatever but a statement of the *meaning* of our assertions about the simultaneity of spatially separated events. Einstein told the physicists (and philosophers): you must first say what you *mean* by simultaneity, and this you can only do by showing how the statement 'two events are simultaneous' is verified. But in so doing you have then also established the meaning fully and *without remainder*. What is true of the simultaneity concept holds good of every other; every statement has a meaning only insofar as it can be verified; it only *signifies* what is verified and absolutely *nothing* beyond this. Were someone to maintain that it contains more, he would have to be able to say what this more is, and for this he must again say what in the world would be different if he was wrong; but he can say nothing of the kind, for by previous assumption all observable differences have already been utilized in the verification.

In the simultaneity example the analysis of meaning, as is right and proper for the physicist, is carried only so far that the decision about the truth or falsity of a temporal statement resides in the occurrence or non-occurrence of a certain physical event (for example, the coincidence of a pointer with a scale-mark); but it is clear that one may go on to ask: What, then, does it *mean* to claim that the pointer indicates a particular mark on the scale? And the answer to this can be nothing else whatever but a reference to the occurrence of certain data, or, as we are wont to say, of certain 'sensations'. This is also generally admitted, and especially by physicists. "For in the end, positivism will always be right in this", says Planck (2), "that there is no other source of knowledge but sensations", and this statement obviously means that the truth or falsity of a physical assertion is quite solely dependent on the occurrence of certain sensations (which are a special class of the given).

But now there will always be many inclined to say that this grants only that the truth of a physical statement can be tested in absolutely no other way save by the occurrence of certain sensations, but that this, however, is a different thing from claiming that the very *meaning* of the statement is thereby exhaustively presented. The latter would have to be denied, for a proposition can contain *more* than allows of verification; that the pointer stands at a certain mark on the scale means *more* than the presence of certain sensations (namely, the 'presence of a certain state-of-affairs in the external world').

Of this denial of the identity of meaning and verification the following needs to be said:

1. Such a denial is to be found among physicists only where they leave the proper territory of physical statements and begin to philosophize. (In physics, obviously, we find only statements about the nature or behaviour of things and processes; an express assertion of their 'reality' is needless, since it is always presupposed.) In his own territory the physicist fully acknowledges the correctness of our point of view. We have already mentioned this earlier, and have since elucidated it by the example of the concept of simultaneity. There are, indeed, many philosophers who say: Only relative simultaneity can admittedly be established, but from this it does not follow that there is no such thing as absolute simultaneity, and we continue, as before, to believe in it! There is no way of demonstrating the falsity of this claim; but the great majority of physicists are rightly of the opinion that it is meaningless. It must be emphatically stressed, however, that in both cases we are concerned with exactly the same situation. It makes absolutely no difference, in principle, whether I ask: Does the statement 'two events are simultaneous' mean more than can be verified? Or whether I ask: Does the statement 'the pointer indicates the fifth scale-mark' signify more than can be verified? The physicist who treats the two cases differently is guilty of an inconsistency. He will justify himself by arguing that in the second case, where the 'reality of the external world' is concerned, there is philosophically far more at stake. This argument is too vague for us to be able to assign it any weight but we shall shortly examine whether anything lies behind it.

2. It is perfectly true that every statement about a phys-

ical object or event says *more* than is verified, say, by the once-and-for-all occurrence of an experience. It is presupposed, rather, that this experience took place under quite specific conditions, whose fulfilment can, of course, be tested in tum only by something given; and it is further presupposed that still other and further verifications (after-tests, confirmations) are always possible, which themselves of course reduce to manifestations of some kind in the given. In this way we can and must make allowance for sense-deceptions and errors, and it is easy to see how we are to classify the cases in which we would say that the observer had merely dreamt that the pointer indicated a certain mark, or that he had not observed carefully, and so on. Blondlot's claims about the N-rays that he thought he had discovered were intended, after all, to say more than that he had had certain visual sensations under certain circumstances, and hence they could also be refuted (3). Strictly speaking, the meaning of a proposition about physical objects is exhausted only by the provision of indefinitely many possible verifications, and the consequence of this is, that in the last resort such a proposition can never be proved absolutely true. It is generally acknowledged, indeed, that even the most assured propositions of science have always to be regarded merely as hypotheses, which remain open to further definition and improvement. This has certain consequences for the logical nature of such propositions, but they do not concern us here.

Once again: the meaning of a physical statement is never defined by a single isolated verification; it must be conceived, rather, as of the form: If circumstances x are given, data y occur, where indefinitely many circumstances can be substituted for x, and the proposition remains correct on every occasion (this also holds, even if the statement refers to a once-and-for-all occurrence — a historical event — for such an event always has innumerable consequences whose occurrence can be verified). Thus the meaning of every physical statement ultimately lies always in an endless chain of data; the individual datum as such is of no interest in this connection. So if a positivist should ever have said that the individual objects of science are simply the given experiences themselves, he would certainly have been quite wrong; what every scientist seeks, and seeks alone, are rather the rules which govern the connection of experiences, and by which they can be predicted. Nobody denies that the sole verification of natural laws consists in the fact that they provide correct predictions of this type. The oft-heard objection, that the immediately given which at most can be the object of psychology, is now falsely to be made into an object of physics, is thereby robbed of its force.

3. The most important thing to say, however, is this: If anyone thinks that the meaning of a proposition is not in fact exhausted by what can be verified in the given, but extends far beyond that, then he must at least admit that this surplus of meaning is utterly indescribable, unstateable in any way, and inexpressible by any language. For let him just try to state it! So far as he succeeds in *communicating* something of the meaning, he will find that the communication consists in the very fact that he has pointed out some circumstances that can serve for verification in the given, and he thereby finds our view confirmed. Or else he may believe, indeed, that he has stated a meaning, but closer examination shows that his words only signify that there is still 'something' there, though nothing whatever is said about its nature. In that case he has really communicated nothing; his claim is meaningless, for one cannot maintain the existence of something without saying of *what* one is claiming the existence. This can be brought out by reference to our example of the essentially indemonstrable 'nucleus of the electron'; but for the sake of clarity we shall analyze yet another example of a very fundamental kind.

I am looking at two pieces of green paper, and establish

that they have the same color. The proposition asserting
the likeness of colour is verified, *inter alia*, by the fact that
I twice experience the same color at the same time. The
statement 'two patches of the same color are now present' can
no longer be reduced to others; it is verified by the fact that
it describes the given. It has a good meaning: by virtue of
the significance of the words occurring in the statement, this
meaning is simply the existence of this similarity of color; by
virtue of linguistic usage, the sentence expresses precisely this
experience. I now show one of the two pieces of paper to a
second observer, and pose the question: Does he see the green
just as I do? Is his color-experience the *same* as mine? This
case is *essentially* different from the one just examined. While
there the statement was verifiable through the occurrence of
an experience of similarity, a brief consideration shows that
here such a verification is absolutely impossible. Of course (if
he is not color-blind), the second observer also calls the paper
green; and if I now describe this green to him more closely,
by saying that it is more yellowish than this wallpaper, more
bluish than this billiard-cloth, darker than this plant and so
on, he will also find it so each time, that is, he will agree with
my statements. But even though all his judgments about
colors were to agree entirely with mine, I can obviously never
conclude from this that he experiences 'the same quality'.
It might be that on looking at the green paper he has an
experience that I should call 'red'; that conversely, in the
cases where I see red, he experiences green, but of course
calls it 'red', and so forth. It might even be, indeed, that
my color sensations are matched in him by experiences of
sound or data of some other kind; yet it would be impossible
in principle ever to dis- cover these differences between his
experience and mine. We would agree completely, and could
never differ about our surroundings, so long only (and this is
absolutely the only precondition that has to be made) as the
inner *order* of his experiences agrees with that of mine. Their

44

'quality' does not come into it at all; all that is required is that they can be brought into a *system* in the same fashion.

All this is doubtless uncontested, and philosophers have pointed out this situation often enough. They have mostly added, however, that such subjective differences are indeed theoretically possible, and that this possibility is in principle very interesting, but that nevertheless it is 'in the highest degree probable' that the observer and I actually experience the *same* green. We, however, must say: The claim that different individuals experience the *same* sensation has this verifiable meaning alone, that all their statements (and of course all their other behavior as well) display certain agreements; hence the claim *means* nothing else whatever but this. It is merely another mode of expression if we say that it is a question of the likeness of two systems of order. The proposition that two experiences of different subjects not only occupy the same place in the order of a system, but *beyond that* are *also* qualitatively like each other, has no meaning for us. It is not false, be it noted, but meaningless: we have no idea at all what it is supposed to signify.

Experience shows that for the majority of people it is very difficult to agree with this. One has to grasp that we are really concerned here with a *logical* impossibility of verification. To speak of the likeness of two data in *the same* consciousness has an acceptable meaning; it can be verified through an immediate experience. But if we wish to talk of the likeness of two data in *different* consciousnesses, that is a new concept; it has to be defined anew, for propositions in which it occurs are no longer verifiable in the old fashion. The new definition is, in fact, the likeness of all reactions of the two individuals; no other can be found. The majority believe, indeed, that no definition is required here; we know straight off what 'like' means, and the meaning is in both cases the same. But in order to recognize this as an error, we have only to recall the concept of simultaneity, where the situation is precisely analogous. To the concept of 'simultaneity at the same place' there corresponds here the concept of 'likeness of experiences in the same individual'; and to 'simultaneity at different places' there corresponds here the 'likeness of experiences in different individuals'. The second is in each case something new in comparison with the first, and must be specially defined. A directly experienceable quality can no more be pointed out for the likeness of two greens in different consciousnesses than for simultaneity at different places; both must be defined by way of a system of relations.

Many philosophers have tried to overcome the difficulty that seemed to confront them here by all sorts of speculations and thought-experiments, in that they have spoken, say, of a universal consciousness (God) embracing all individuals, or have imagined that perhaps by an artificial linkage of the nerve-systems of two people the sensations of the one might be made accessible to the other and could be compared — but all this is useless, of course, since even by such fantastical methods it is in the end only contents of one and the same consciousness that are directly compared; but the question is precisely whether a comparison is possible between qualities insofar as they belong to different consciousnesses, and *not* the same one.

It must be admitted, therefore, that a proposition about the likeness of the experiences of two different persons has no other *stateable* meaning save that of a certain agreement in their reactions. Now it is open to anyone to believe that such a proposition also possesses another, more direct meaning; but it is certain that this meaning is not verifiable, and that there can be no way at all of stating or pointing out what this meaning is supposed to be. From this it follows, however, that there is absolutely no way at all in which such a meaning could be made a topic of discussion; there could be absolutely no talk about it, and it can in no way enter into any language whereby we communicate with each other.

And what has, we hope, become clear from this example, is of quite general application. All we can understand in a proposition is what it conveys; but a meaning can be communicated only if it is verifiable. Since propositions are nothing else but a vehicle of communication we can assign to their meaning only what can be communicated. For this reason I should insist that 'meaning' can never signify anything but 'stateable meaning'.

But even if someone insisted that there was a nonverifiable meaning, this would actually be of no consequence whatever; for in everything he says and asks, and in everything that we ask him and reply to him, *such* a meaning can never in any way come to light. In other words, if such a thing were to exist, all our utterances and arguments and modes of behavior would still remain totally untouched by it, whether it was a question of daily life, of ethical or aesthetic attitude, of science of any kind, or of philosophy. Everything would be exactly as though there were no unverifiable meaning, for insofar as anything was different, it would in fact be verifiable through this very difference.

That is a serious situation, and we must absolutely demand that it be taken seriously. One must guard above all things against confusing the present logical impossibility with an empirical incapacity, just as though some technical difficulties and human imperfection were to blame for the fact that only the verifiable can be expressed, and as though there were still some little backdoor through which an unstateable meaning could slip into the daylight and make itself noticeable in our speech and behavior! No! The incommunicability is an absolute one; anyone who believes in a nonverifiable meaning (or more accurately, we shall have to say, imagines he believes in this) must still confess that only *one* attitude remains in regard to it: absolute silence. It would be of no use either to him or us, however often he asserted: 'but there is a non-verifiable meaning', for this statement is itself devoid of meaning, and says nothing.

III. What Does 'Reality' Mean? What Does 'external World' Mean?

We are now prepared to make application of the foregoing to the so-called problem of the reality of the external world,

Let us ask: What meaning has it, if the 'realist' says 'there is an external world'? or even: What meaning attaches to the claim (which the realist attributes to the positivist) 'there is no external world'?

To answer the question, it is necessary, of course, to clarify the significance of the words 'there is' and 'external world'. Let us begin with the first. 'There is x amounts to saying 'x is real' or 'x is actual'. So what does it mean if we attribute actuality (or reality) to an object? It is an ancient and very important insight of logic or philosophy, that the proposition 'x is actual' is totally different in kind from a proposition that attributes any sort of *property* to x (such as 'x is hard'). In other words, actuality, reality or existence is not a property. The statement 'the dollar in my pocket is round' has a totally different logical form from the statement 'the dollar in my pocket is actual'. In modern logic this distinction is expressed by an altogether different symbolism, but it had already been very sharply emphasized by Kant, who, as we know, in his critique of the so-called ontological proof of God's existence had correctly found the error of this proof in the fact that existence was treated like a property there.

In daily life we very often have to speak of actuality or existence, and for that very reason it cannot be hard to discover the meaning of this talk. In a legal battle it often has to be established whether some document really exists, or whether this has merely been falsely claimed, say, by one of the parties; nor is it wholly unimportant to me, whether the dollar in my pocket is merely imaginary or actually real. Now everybody knows in what way such a reality-claim is verified, nor can there be the least doubt about it; the reality of the dollar is proved by this, and this alone, that by suitable manipulations I furnish myself certain tactual or visual sensations, on whose occurrence I am accustomed to say: this is a dollar. The same holds of the document, only there we should be content, on occasion, with certain statements by others claiming to have seen the document, that is, to have had perceptions of a quite specific kind. And the 'statements of others' again consist in certain acoustic, or — if they were written utterances — visual perceptions, There is need of no special controversy about the fact that the occurrence of certain sense-perceptions among the data *always* constitutes the sole criterion for propositions about the reality of a 'physical' object or event, in daily life no less than in the most refined assertions of science. That there are okapis in Africa can be established only by observing such animals. But it is not necessary that the object or event 'itself' should have to be perceived, We can imagine, for example, that the existence of a trans-Neptunian planet might be inferred by observation of perturbations with just as much certainty as by direct perception of a speck of light in the telescope. The reality of the atom provides another example, as does the back side of the moon.

It is of great importance to state that the occurrence of some one particular experience in verifying a reality-statement is often not recognized as such a verification, but that it is throughout a question of regularities, of law-like connections; in this way true verifications are distinguished from illusions and hallucinations. If we say of some event or object — which must be marked out by a description — that it is *real*, this means, then, that there is a quite specific connection between perceptions or other experiences, that under given circumstances certain data are presented. By this alone is it verified, and hence this is also its only stateable meaning.

This, too, was already formulated, in principle, by Kant,

whom nobody will accuse of 'positivism'. Reality, for him, is a category, and if we apply it anywhere, and claim of an object that it is real, then all this asserts, in Kant's opinion, is that it belongs to a law-governed connection of perceptions.

It will be seen that for us (as for Kant; and the same must apply to any philosopher who is aware of his task) it is merely a matter of saying what is meant when we ascribe real existence to a thing in life or in science; it is in no sense a matter of correcting the claims of ordinary life or of research. I must confess that I should charge with folly and reject *a limine* every philosophical system that involved the claim that clouds and stars, mountains and the sea, were not actually real, that the 'physical world' did not exist, and that the chair against the wall ceases to be every time I tum my back on it, Nor do I seriously impute such a claim to any thinker. It would, for example, be undoubtedly a quite mistaken account of Berkeley's philosophy if his system were to be understood in this fashion. He, too, in no way denied the reality of the physical world, but merely sought to explain what we mean when we attribute reality to it. Anyone who says here that unperceived things are ideas in the mind of God is not in fact denying their existence, but is seeking, rather, to understand it. Even John Stuart Mill was not wanting to deny the reality of physical objects, but rather to explain it, when he declared them to be 'permanent possibilities of sensation', although I do consider his mode of expression to have been very unsuitably chosen.

So if 'positivism' is understood to mean a view that denies reality to bodies, I should simply have to declare it absurd; but I do not believe that such an interpretation of positivist opinions, at least as regards their competent exponents, would be historically just. Yet, however that may be, we are concerned only with the issue itself. And on this we have established as follows: our principle, that the question about the meaning of a proposition is identical with the question about its verification, leads us to recognize that the claim that a thing is real is a statement about lawful connections of experiences; it does *not*, however, imply this claim to be false. (There is therefore no denial of reality to physical objects in favor of sensations.)

But opponents of the view presented profess themselves by no means satisfied with this assertion. So far as I can see, they would answer as follows: 'You do, indeed, acknowledge completely the reality of the physical world, but — as we see it — only in words. You simply *call* real what we should describe as mere conceptual constructions. When *we* use the word "reality", we mean by it something quite different from you. Your definition of the real reduces it to experiences; but we mean something quite independent of all experiences. We mean something that possesses the same independence that you obviously concede only to the data, in that you reduce everything else to them, as the not-further-reducible'.

Although it would be a sufficient rebuttal to request our opponents to reflect once more upon how reality-statements are verified, and how verification is connected with *meaning*, I do in fact recognize the need to take account of the psychological attitude from which this argument springs, and therefore beg attention to the following considerations, whereby a modification of this attitude may yet, perhaps, be effected.

Let us first enquire whether, on our view, a 'content of consciousness' is credited with a reality that is denied to a physical object. We ask, therefore: does the claim that a feeling or sensation is real have a meaning different from the claim that a physical object is real? For us, this can mean only: are different types of verification involved in the two cases? The answer is: no!

To clarify this, we need to enter a little into the logical form of reality-statements. The general logical recognition that an existence-statement can be made about a datum only if it is marked out by a description, but not if it is given by an immediate indication, is also valid, of course, for the 'data of consciousness'. In the language of symbolic logic, this is expressed by the fact that an existence-claim must contain an 'operator'. In Russell's notation, for example, a reality-statement has the form $(\exists x)fx$, or in words, 'there is an x that has the property f'. The form of words 'there is a', where 'a' is supposed to be the individual name of a directly indicated object, therefore means no more than 'this here'; this form of words is meaningless, and in Russell's symbolism it cannot even be written down. We have to grasp the idea that Descartes's proposition 'I am' — or, to put it better, 'contents of consciousness exist' — is absolutely meaningless; it expresses nothing, and contains no knowledge. This is due to the fact that 'contents of consciousness' occurs in this connection as a mere *name* for the given; no characteristic is asserted, whose presence could be tested. A proposition has meaning, and is verifiable, only if I can state under what circumstances it would be true, and under what circumstances it would be false. But how am I to describe the circumstances under which the proposition 'My contents of consciousness exist' would be false? Every attempt would lead to ridiculous absurdities, to such propositions, say, as 'It is the case that nothing is the case', or the like. Hence I am self-evidently unable to describe the circumstances that make the proposition true (just try it!). Nor is there any doubt whatever that Descartes, with his proposition, had really obtained no knowledge, and was actually no wiser than before.

No, the question about the reality of an experience has meaning only where this reality can also be meaningfully *doubted*. I can ask, for example: Is it really true that I felt joy on hearing that news? This can be verified or falsified exactly as when we ask, say: Is it true that Sirius has a companion (that this companion is real)? That I felt joy on a particular occasion can be verified, for example, by examination of other people's statements about my behaviour at the time, by my finding of a letter that I then wrote, or simply by the return to me of an exact memory of the emotion I experienced. Here, therefore, there is not the slightest difference of principle: to be real always means to stand in a definite connection with the given. Nor is it otherwise, say, with an experience that is present at this very moment. I can quite meaningfully ask, for example (in the course, say, of a physiological experiment): Do I now actually feel a pain or not? (Notice that 'pain', here, does not function as an individual name for a 'this here', but represents a conceptual term for a describable class of experiences.) Here, too, the question is answered by establishing that in conjunction with certain circumstances (experimental conditions, concentration of attention, etc.) an experience with certain describable properties occurs. Such describable properties would be, for example: similarity to an experience that has occurred under certain other circumstances; tendency to evoke certain reactions; and so on.

However we may twist and turn, it is impossible to interpret a reality-statement otherwise than as fitting into a perceptual context. It is absolutely the *same* kind of reality that we have to attribute to the data of consciousness and to physical events. Scarcely anything in the history of philosophy has created more confusion than the attempt to pick out one of the two as true 'being'. Wherever the term 'real' is intelligibly used, it has one and the same meaning.

Our opponent, perhaps, will still feel his position unshaken by what we have said, having the impression, rather, that the arguments here presented presuppose a starting-point at which he cannot, from the outset, station himself. He has to concede that the decision about the reality or unreality of anything in experience takes place, in every case, in the manner outlined, but he claims that in this way we only arrive at what Kant called *empirical* reality. It designates the area governed by the observations of daily life and of science, but beyond this boundary there lies something else, *transcendent* reality, which cannot be inferred by strict logic, and is thus no postulate of the understanding, though it is a postulate of sound *reason*. It is the only true *external world*, and this alone is at issue in the philosophical problem of the existence of the external world. The discussion thereupon abandons the question about the meaning of the term 'reality', and turns to that about the meaning of the term 'external world'.

The term 'external world' is obviously used in two different ways: firstly in the usage of daily life, and secondly as a technical term in philosophy.

Where it occurs in everyday life, it has, like the majority of expressions employed in practical affairs, an intelligibly stateable meaning. In contrast to the 'internal world', which covers memories, thoughts, dreams, wishes and feelings, the 'external world' means nothing else, here, but the world of mountains and trees, houses, animals and men. What it means to maintain the existence of a certain object in this world, is known to every child; and it was necessary to point out that it really means absolutely nothing *more* than what the child knows. We all know how to verify the proposition, say, that 'There is a Castle in the park before the town'. We perform certain acts, and if certain exactly specifiable states-of-affairs come about, then we say: 'Yes, there really is a Castle there'; otherwise we say: 'That statement was an error or a lie'. And if somebody now asks us: 'But was the Castle there in the night as well, when nobody saw it?' we answer: 'Undoubtedly! for it would have been impossible to build it in the period from early this morning till now, and besides, the state of the building shows that it was not only already *in situ* yesterday, but has been there for a hundred years, and hence since before we were born'. We are thus in possession of quite specific empirical criteria for whether houses and trees were also there when we were not seeing them, and whether they already existed before our birth, and will exist after our death. That is to say, the claim that these things 'exist independently of us' has a perfectly clear, testable meaning, and is obviously to be answered in the affirmative. We are very well able to distinguish such things in a stateable way from those that only occur 'subjectively', 'in dependence upon ourselves'. If, owing to an eye defect, I see, for example, a dark speck when I look at the wall opposite me, I say of it that it is there only when I look, whereas I say of the wall that it is also there when I am not looking. The verification of this difference is in fact very easy, and both claims assert precisely what is contained in these verifications and nothing more.

So if the term 'external world' is taken in the everyday sense, the question about its existence simply means: Are there, in addition to memories, wishes and ideas, also stars, clouds, plants and animals, and my own body? We have just affirmed once more that it would be utterly absurd to say no to this question. There are obviously houses and clouds and animals existing independently of us, and I have already said earlier that a thinker who denied the existence of the external world in this sense would have no claim to our attention. Instead of telling us what we mean when we speak of mountains and plants, he wishes to persuade us that there are no such things at all!

But now how about science? When it speaks of the external world, does it, unlike daily life, mean something other than things such as houses and trees? It seems to me that this is by no means the case. For atoms and electric fields, or whatever else the physicist may speak of, are precisely what houses and trees consist of, according to his teaching; the one must therefore be real in the same sense as the other. The objectivity of mountains and clouds is just exactly the same as that of protons and energies; the latter stand in no greater contrast to the 'subjectivity' of feelings, say, or hallucinations, than do the former. We have long since convinced ourselves, in fact, that the existence of even the most subtle of the 'invisible' things postulated by the scientist is verified, in principle, in exactly the same way as the reality of a tree or a star.

In order to settle the dispute about realism, it is of the greatest importance to alert the physicist to the fact that his external world is nothing else but the *nature* which also surrounds us in daily life, and is not the 'transcendent world' of the metaphysicians. The difference between the two is again quite particularly evident in the philosophy of Kant. Nature, and everything of which the physicist can and must speak, belongs, in Kant's view, to empirical reality, and the meaning of this (as already mentioned) is explained by him exactly as we have also had to do. Atoms, in Kant's system, have no transcendent reality — they are not 'things-in-themselves'. Thus the physicist cannot appeal to the Kantian philosophy; his arguments lead only to the empirical external world that we all acknowledge, not to a transcendent one; his electrons are not metaphysical entities.

Many scientists speak, nonetheless, of the necessity of having to postulate the existence of an external world as a *metaphysical* hypothesis. They never do this, indeed, within their own science (although all the necessary hypotheses of a science ought to occur *within it*), but only at the point where they leave this territory and begin to philosophize. The transcendent external world is actually something that is referred to exclusively in philosophy, never in a science or in daily life. It is simply a technical term, whose meaning we now have to inquire into.

How does the transcendent or metaphysical external world differ from the empirical one? In philosophical systems it is thought of as subsisting somehow behind the empirical world, where the word 'behind' is also supposed to indicate that this world is not *knowable* in the same sense as the empirical, that it lies beyond a boundary that divides the accessible from the inaccessible.

This distinction originally has its ground in the view formerly shared by the majority of philosophers, that to know an object requires that it be immediately given directly experienced; knowledge is a kind of intuition, and is perfect only if the known is directly present to the knower, like a sensation or a feeling. So what cannot be immediately experienced or intuited remains, on this view, unknowable, ungraspable, transcendent, and belongs to the realm of things-in-themselves. Here, as I have elsewhere had to state on numerous occasions, we simply have a confusion of knowing with mere acquaintance or experiencing. But such a confusion is certainly not committed by modern scientists; I do not believe that any physicist considers knowledge of the electron to consist in its entering bodily, by an act of intuition, into the scientist's consciousness; he will take the view, rather, that for complete knowledge the only thing needed is for the regularity of an electron's behaviour to be so exhaustively stated that all formulae in which its properties occur in any way are totally confirmed by experience. In other words, the electron, and all physical realities likewise, are *not* unknowable things-in-themselves, and do not belong to a transcendent, metaphysical reality, if this is characterized by the fact that it embraces the unknowable.

Thus we again return to the conclusion that all the physicist's hypotheses can relate only to *empirical* reality, if by this we mean the knowable. It would in fact be a self-contradiction to wish to assume something unknowable as a hypothesis. For there must always be specific *reasons* for setting up a hypothesis, since it is, after all, supposed to fulfil a specific purpose. What is assumed in the hypothesis must therefore have the property of fulfilling this purpose, and of being precisely so constituted as to be justified by these reasons. But in virtue of this very fact certain statements are made of it, and these contain *knowledge* of it. And they contain, indeed, *complete* knowledge of it, since *only* that can be hypothetically assumed for which there are reasons in experience.

Or does the scientific 'realist' wish to characterize the talk of not immediately experienced objects as a metaphysical hypothesis for some reason other than the nonexistent one of its unknowability? To this, perhaps, he will answer 'yes'. In fact it can be seen from numerous statements in the literature, that the physicist by no means couples his claim of a transcendent world with the claim that it is unknowable; on the contrary, he (quite rightly) takes the view that the nature of extra-mental things is reflected with perfect correctness in his equations. Hence the external world of the physical realist is not that of traditional metaphysics. He employs the technical term of the philosophers, but what he designates by means of it has seemed to us to be merely the external world of everyday life, whose existence is doubted by nobody, not even the 'positivist'.

So what is this other reason that leads the 'realist' to regard his external world as a metaphysical assumption? Why does he want to distinguish it from the empirical external world that we have described? The answer to this question leads us back again to an earlier point in our argument. For the 'realistic' physicist is perfectly content with our description of the external world, except on one point: he thinks that we have not lent it enough *reality*. It is not by its unknowability or any other feature that he takes his 'external world' to differ from the empirical one; it is simply and solely by the fact that another, higher reality attaches to it. This often finds expression even in the terminology; the word 'real' is often reserved for this external world, in contrast to the merely 'ideal', 'subjective' content of consciousness, and the mere 'logical constructions' into which 'positivism' is accused of dissolving reality.

But now even the physical realist has a dim feeling that, as we know, reality is not a 'property'; hence he cannot simply pass from our empirical external world to his transcendent one by attributing to it the feature of 'reality' over and above the features that we, too, ascribe to all physical objects; yet that is how he talks, and this illegitimate leap, whereby he leaves the realm of the meaningful, would in fact be 'metaphysical', and is also felt to be such by himself.

We now have a clear view of the situation, and can judge it on the basis of the preceding considerations.

Our principle, that the truth and falsity of all statements, including those about the reality of a physical object, can be tested only in the 'given', and that *therefore* the meaning of all statements can likewise be formulated and understood only by means of the given — this principle has been wrongly construed as if it claimed or presupposed that only the given is real. Hence the 'realist' feels compelled to contradict the principle, and to set up the counterclaim, that the meaning of a reality-statement is by no means exhausted in mere assertions of the form 'Under these particular circumstances this particular experience will occur' (where these assertions, on our view, are in any case an infinite multitude); the meaning, he says, in fact lies *beyond this* in something else, which must be referred to, say, as 'independent existence', 'transcendent being' or the like, and of which our principle provides no account.

To this we ask: Well, then, *how* does one give an account of it? What do these words 'independent existence' and 'transcendent being' mean? In other words, what testable difference does it make in the world, whether an object has transcendent being or not?

Two answers are given here. The first runs: It makes a quite enormous difference. For a scientist who believes in a 'real external world' will feel and work quite differently from one who merely aims at 'describing sensations'. The former will regard the starry heaven, whose aspect recalls to him the inconceivable sublimity and size of the universe, and his own human smallness, with feelings of awe and devotion quite different from those of the latter, to whom the most distant galactic systems are but 'complexes of his own sensations.' The first will be devoted to his task with an enthusiasm, and will feel in his knowing of the objective world a satisfaction, that are denied to the second, since he takes himself to be concerned only with constructions of his own.

To this first answer we have this to say: If, in the behaviour of two thinkers, there should anywhere occur a difference such as has here been described — and it would in fact involve an observable state-of-affairs — and were we to insist upon so expressing this difference as to say that the first believes in a real external world, and the other not — well, even so, the *meaning* of our assertion still consists solely in what we observe in the behavior of the two. That is to say, the words 'absolute reality', or 'transcendent being', or whatever other terms we may use for it, now *signify* absolutely nothing else but certain states of feeling which arise in the two whenever they contemplate the universe, or make reality-statements, or philosophize. The fact of the matter is, that employment of the words 'independent existence', 'transcendent reality' and so on, is simply and solely the expression of a feeling, a psychological attitude of the speaker (which may in the end, moreover, apply to all metaphysical propositions). If someone assures us that there is a real external world in the supra-empirical sense of the term, he thinks, no doubt, that he has thereby conveyed a truth about the world; but in actuality his words express a quite different state-of-affairs, namely the mere presence of certain feelings, which provoke him to specific reactions of a verbal or other nature.

If the self-evident still needs to be specially dwelt on, I should like to underline — but in that case with maximum emphasis, and with stress upon the *seriousness* of what I am saying — that the nonmetaphysician does not differ from the metaphysician by the fact, say, that he lacks those feelings to which the other gives expression by way of the propositions of a 'realistic' philosophy, but only by the fact that he has recognized that these propositions by no means have the meaning that they seem to have, and are therefore to be avoided. He will give expression to the same feelings in a *different* way. In other words, this confrontation of the two types of thinker, set up in the realist's first answer, was misleading and erroneous. If anyone is so unfortunate as not to feel the sublimity of the starry heaven, then the blame lies on something other than a logical analysis of the concepts of reality and the external world. To suppose that the opponent of metaphysics is incapable, say, of justly estimating the greatness of Copernicus, because in a certain sense the Ptolemaic view reflects the empirical situation just as well as the Copernican, seems to me no less strange than to believe that the 'positivist' cannot be a good father to his family, because according to his theory his children are merely complexes of his own sensations, and it is therefore senseless to make provision for their welfare after his death. No, the world of the non-metaphysician is the same world as that of everybody else; it lacks nothing that is needed in order to make meaningful all the statements of science and all the actions of daily life. He merely refuses to add meaningless statements to his description of the world.

We come to the *second* answer that can be given to the question about the meaning of the claim that there is a transcendent reality. It simply consists in admitting that it makes absolutely no difference for experience whether we postulate something else existing behind the empirical world or not; metaphysical realism cannot therefore be actually tested or verified. Thus it cannot be further stated what is meant by this claim; yet something *is* meant thereby, and the meaning can also be understood without verification.

This is nothing else but the view criticized in the previous Section, that the meaning of a proposition has nothing to do with its verification, and it only remains for us to repeat once more our earlier general criticism, as applied to this particular Case. We must reply, therefore: Well now! You are giving the name 'existence' or 'reality' here to something that is utterly inexpressible and cannot be explained or stated in any fashion. You think, nonetheless, that these words have a meaning. As to that, we shall not quarrel with you. But this much is certain: by the admission just made, this meaning cannot in any way become manifest, cannot be expressed by any oral or written communication, or by any gesture or act. For if this were possible, a testable empirical situation would exist; there would be something *different* in the world, if the proposition 'There is a transcendent world' were true, from if it were false. This differentness would then signify the meaning of the words 'real external world' and hence it would be an empirical meaning — that is, this real external world would again be merely the empirical world which we, too, acknowledge, like everyone else. Even to speak, merely, of another world, is logically impossible. There can be no discussion about it, for a nonverifiable existence cannot enter as meaning into any possible proposition. Anyone who still believes in such a thing — or imagines he believes — can only do so in silence. There are arguments only for something that can be said. The results of our discussion can be summarized as follows:

1. The principle, that the meaning of every proposition is exhaustively determined by its verification in the given, seems to me a legitimate, unassailable core of the 'positivist' schools of thought.

But within these schools it has seldom come clearly to light, and has often been mingled with so many untenable principles, that a logical clean-up is necessary. If we want to call the result of this clean-up 'positivism', which might well be justified on historical grounds, we should have, perhaps, to affix a differentiating adjective: the term (4) 'logical' or 'logistic positivism' is often used; otherwise the expression 'consistent empiricism' has seemed to me appropriate.

2. This principle does not mean, nor does it follow from

it, that only the given is real; such a claim would actually be meaningless.

3. Consistent empiricism, therefore, does *not* deny, either, the existence of an external world; it merely points out the empirical meaning of this existence-claim.

4. It is not an 'as if theory'. It does not say, for example, that everything behaves as if there were physical independent bodies; on the contrary, for it, too, everything is real that the nonphilosophizing scientist declares to be real. The subject matter of physics does not consist of sensations, but of laws. The formulation employed by some positivists, that bodies are mere 'complexes of sensations' is therefore to be rejected. The only correct view is that propositions about bodies can be transformed into propositions of like meaning about the regularity of occurrence of sensations (5).

5. Logical positivism and realism are therefore not opposed; anyone who ac- knowledges our principle must actually be an empirical realist.

6. There is opposition only between consistent empiricism and the metaphysician, and it is directed as much against the realist as the Idealist (the former is designated in our discussion as a 'realist', in quotation-marks).

7. The denial of the existence of a transcendent external world would be just as much a metaphysical proposition as its assertion; the consistent empiricist does not therefore deny the transcendent, but declares both its denial and its affirmation to be equally devoid of meaning.

This last distinction is of the greatest importance. I am convinced that the main resistances to our viewpoint stem from the fact that the difference between the falsity and the meaninglessness of a proposition is not heeded. The proposition 'Talk of a metaphysical external world is meaningless' does *not* say 'There is no metaphysical external world', but something *toto coelo* different. The empiricist does not say to the metaphysician: 'Your words assert something false', but

'Your words assert nothing at all!' He does not contradict the metaphysician, but says: 'I do not understand you'.

Notes

1. [E. Laas, *Idealismus und Positivismus, Eine kritische Auseinanderseizung.* Berlin 1879-1881.]
2. M. Planck, *Positivismus und reale Aussenwelt*, Leipzig 1931, p. 14.
3. Cf. *ibid.*, p. 11.
4. Cf. the article by A. E. Blumberg and H. Feigl ["Logical Positivism"] in *The Journal of Philosophy* **28** (1931); see also E. Kaila ['Der logistische Neupositinsmus. Eine kritische Studie'] in *Annales Universitatis Aboensis* **13** (1930), and A. Petzall ["Logistischer Positivismus"] in *Göreborgs Högskolas Arsskrift* **37** (1931).
5. On this, as on the content of the whole essay, cf. the article by H. Cornelius ['Zur Kritik der wissenschaftlichen Grundbegriffe'] in *Erkenntnis* **2** (1931). The formulations there are admittedly not free from objection. Cf. also the outstanding discussion by Philipp Frank in chapter X of his book *Das Kausalgesetz und seine Grenzen*, Wien 1932, and Rudolf Carnap, *Scheinprobleme in der Philosophie*, Leipzig and Berlin 1928.